Building Blocks for Planning Functional Library Space

Library Leadership & Management Association
American Library Association

Third Edition

The American Library Association
and
THE SCARECROW PRESS, INC.
Lanham • Toronto • Plymouth, UK
2011

Published by Scarecrow Press, Inc.
A wholly owned subsidiary of The Rowman & Littlefield Publishing Group, Inc.
4501 Forbes Boulevard, Suite 200, Lanham, Maryland 20706
http://www.scarecrowpress.com

Estover Road, Plymouth PL6 7PY, United Kingdom

British Library Cataloguing in Publication Information Available

Library of Congress Cataloging-in-Publication Data

Building blocks for planning functional library space / Library Leadership & Management
Association, American Library Association. — 3rd ed.
 p. cm.
 Summary: "With drawings of typical furniture and equipment, along with diagrams
required for their use, this expanded and revised edition of Building Blocks helps planners
design new, renovated, or existing library space"— Provided by publisher.
 Includes bibliographical references.
 ISBN 978-0-8108-8104-4 (pbk.)
 1. Libraries—Space utilization. 2. Library fittings and supplies. I. Library Leadership and
Management Association.
 Z679.55.B85 2011
 022'.9—dc23   2011027911

 The paper used in this publication meets the minimum requirements of American National
Standard for Information Sciences—Permanence of Paper for Printed Library Materials,
ANSI/NISO Z39.48-1992.

Printed in the United States of America

Table of Contents

INTRODUCTION
WHAT IS THIS BOOK ABOUT?

This book is unique in providing drawings of typical library furniture and equipment together with diagrams of the space required for their use. Using the square footages recommended in *Building Blocks*, planners of new, renovated, or existing space will be better able to effectively utilize the space they have and to resist the temptation to overload a given space with too many functions.

Although the diagrams and their use are the primary focus of the book, the brief text provides an overview of the planning process. The text also offers detail on several aspects of the planning and design process which the authors have found to be particularly challenging in their own experience.

WHO IS THIS BOOK FOR?

This book is for you if you have any involvement with space planning. You may be the only planner in a one-room library, in which case this book may be all you need because much of the task is clearly visible to you. You may be a department head in a very large library, responsible for meeting with architects about the layout of your department's new or renovated workspace, in which case the architects and planners may provide most of the framework. This book may help you think about the issues that the architects will raise, and can give you an idea of how your contribution fits in to the whole. If you are somewhere between these extremes you may need resources beyond this book, but it can provide an outline for your space planning process and the bibliography can lead you to books and articles that will take you deeper into the library design process.

WHERE ELSE CAN I FIND INFORMATION?

The one publication that best complements this book is the *Checklist of Library Building Design Considerations*, by William Sannwald, listed in the bibliography. It provides the next level of detail in the form of thousands of questions to help you think of the smaller building blocks.

THE PLANNING PROCESS

Extensive institutional planning can take several years and address myriad issues beyond the scope of this book, but the fundamental steps are the same regardless of the scale of the project. Most planning processes include the four elements listed below.

1.   Identify goals

What do you want to accomplish in the new or rearranged space? The problems with your current space are probably at the front of your mind, plus particular goals for numbers of seats, workstations, or volumes. However, this is the time to think of the new space, and set design goals for it. Think of the ways that society and libraries are changing. Touch base with your users, either informally or by using focus groups and community meetings. See what other libraries are doing. What went well for them? What didn't? What may have worked for them but may not be suitable for you? Talk to your colleagues, administrators, and people in the spaces and functions near you.

2.   Define the limits of the project

Probably you will first think of the physical limits (the walls, columns and such) and the budget. Other limits may be the amount of time you and your staff can spend on planning, and whether you have access to professionals and consultants.

3.   Know and understand the existing conditions

Unless you are doing the project by yourself, the professionals or the larger team should be involved in reviewing the existing conditions. If you are rearranging or minimally remodeling an existing space, obtain or draw a scaled plan of the area of the project. Use an architectural plan if you have one available, or use 1/4" or 1/8" graph paper, with each square representing one square foot. Show columns, windows, and other fixed elements that will constrain the layout of the remodeled or rearranged space. Show doors and the circulation spaces (halls or aisles) leading to the exits. Show the locations of present electrical and phone/data outlets.

You may find that once you have the floor plan, just sketching in the area of existing services and collections is sufficient. Or, you can use a photocopier to enlarge or reduce the diagrams in this book to place on the floor plan. Also count and/or describe the existing materials and services that are to go into the new space. If there are items in your current space that will **not** be in the new space, mark these on your plan.

As the planning proceeds you may want to propose moving or removing walls and outlets. It will help to have a plan that you can point to. The plan will also keep you and those who work on the project with you aware of all of the components of your service.

4.   Develop planning options
These can be in the form of statements, sketches, or plans. Is your project limited to rearranging the furniture and shelving? If so, new ADA (Americans with Disabilities Act) regulations may apply, and the floor load capacity will need to be checked in the area where the shelving is to be located. Will you be able to move or add electrical outlets and data jacks? If so, the difficulty of getting into the walls or limits of capacity in the electrical or data panels may be an issue. Will you be able to move walls or add space? If so, your specific ideas or sketches will be helpful in communicating with architects or planners.

This is also the time for you to record your ideas about the new materials and services that are to go into the space, in the form of statements, sketches, or plans. If your library is planning a major renovation or a new facility, your contribution at this point may be primarily quantitative—the number of public workstations, reader seats, staff offices and workstations, volumes to house, copiers, and other items.

You will begin to think of details that you want to keep track of—do you want a pencil-rim on the back of the computer desks, to keep the users' small items from falling down into the cables and plugs below the work surface? Begin to keep these notes in one place, not embedded in meeting notes or other fugitive documents, so that you will be able to refer to them at the right time in the planning process.

WHERE ARE YOU IN THE PROCESS?
The three major starting points are: 1) planning for new construction, where the shape, size, and layout of the new space are all unknown; 2) remodeling an existing space, where the shape and size of the space are known, but not the internal layout; and 3) rearranging within an existing space, where the overall shape of the space is known, and some major elements may not be moved, but some elements will be rearranged to create more space for some functions or to change the flow of work or service. An example would be moving some books out of a branch library to remote storage in order to create more space for study or computer use.

The first stages of planning are the same wherever you are starting. The difference is the degree of freedom you and the planning team have in getting to the outcome. In any case, you and the planners you work with will think about programs (what you want to put in the space), adjacency diagrams (what goes next to what), and flow diagrams (how you want people and materials to move from one space to another, for example; should Acquisitions or Serials be closer to the mail room door?)

Even if you are only rearranging the user furniture in a branch library, it is helpful to think beyond the carpet-edge of the reading area to see if the relationship of the surrounding services can be improved. Perhaps you will see that it can and you will be able to make the case for that.

DOING THE PLANNING YOURSELF
Armed with floor plans, the diagrams in this book, and drawings of your specialized furniture or service desks, you can make your own floor plans for small projects.

You will usually be able to rearrange staff or user furniture as long as you do not encroach on the main aisle ways leading to exits. You will usually be able to move or add electrical outlets and phone/data jacks without involving a planner or a consultant. The electrician who is to do the work can usually determine whether there is enough power available to add outlets or to see if power can be routed to your desired locations.

However, in these days of ADA requirements and more detailed life safety codes, even simple rearrangements can require hiring or consulting one or more code consultants to review your plans.

Any added book stacks must be compatible with your local ADA requirements. Any major renovation or major rearrangement of a space (especially of book stacks) can "trigger" a requirement that the **entire** facility be rearranged with wider stack aisles to comply with ADA. Your local ADA authority will decide what is "major."

Most renovations will trigger a need to review the plans for compliance with the current fire code. Even a rearrangement of the contents of a space requires fire code review to ensure that there is adequate aisle space appropriately located for access to fire exits.

WORKING WITH A PLANNER

Your project architect or space planner is less familiar with your library and its uses than you are. Often this person is not an expert on library services. However, an architect or space planner is an expert in his own field, and brings a fresh view to your space and services. You can make the most of the collaboration with a three-pronged approach.

First, have goals. What are you doing and for whom? What do you most need to accomplish, or to fix? Do you have ideas about the layout of the new space? If so, make some sketches—they don't have to be professional. Have you conducted focus groups or community meetings? If not, do you want your planning partner to do these with you?

Second, understand your way of thinking. Often there are major communication difficulties between library staffers and space planners because library staff are more likely to think and communicate in terms of written or spoken words. Space planners are more likely to think in terms of spaces, as conveyed by drawings, sketches, and gestures. In a meeting with a space planner, often the library participant is talking or pointing to a written document, and the space planner is sketching or waving his arms.

If you see yourself as not being the floor-plan type, you and the planner may be able to reach common ground by going to an example of the space being planned (such as a service desk or staff work space) and walking through the process that occurs there. Often this kinesthetic thinking will work for both of you. If you are at a service desk, show the space planner where you stand, where the library user stands, where you put the materials you are both looking at, where the user puts her backpack or materials, and what you need to be able to reach during the transaction. If you act out or pantomime the transaction, it will help both of you see how much space is needed, the height of surfaces, the location of drawers and keyboards, etc. If it is a staff space, show the space planner where the book truck goes, where the staff person puts the item being worked on, and how the materials being processed are moved into and out of the space.

Third, get your money's worth by picking your planner's brain before you offer your specific ideas ("I thought we'd put the service desk over there…"). If you present your plan first, you may not get to see what the planner can come up with.

In short: don't give up your goals, and make sure your operations are understood. Many of your library colleagues have sad stories about the service desk that is too big or too small or too far from the entrance or the work spaces that do not have room for an adjacent book truck or small work table. Often the space planner never "sees" the space in terms of its function. The illustrations later in this book can help you show him how much space certain functions take, but make sure the space planner understands the flow of people or work product.

PLANNING DOCUMENTS: PROGRAM PLANS

Architects and space planners use a number of devices in their work. The one you are probably most familiar with is the floor plan, which comes fairly late in the design process. The diagrams that compose the majority of this book include small parts of floor plans. Other planning devices may be less familiar to you, and many projects do not include all of the following types of planning devices.

The first of these planning devices is the **program plan**, also sometimes called the **building program**, or just the **program**. Most projects include a program plan. The program plan is a text document that describes the functions within the library and the space requirements of each. The program first lists all of the major spaces (circulation, collections, reader seats, staff areas, etc.), then within each area lists all of the space-consuming items (study seat, workstation, circulation desk, etc.), how many of each are to be in the space, and the square footage needed for each.

The program plan may be done by the architect, but it is often done by a library building consultant and often completed before an architect is selected. Programming is considered a "pre-design" function because the program shows "how many and how much," not the specific look of the building or of the spaces within it.

During the program planning stage library representatives work with the consultant or architect to identify the uses of the new space, first on a large scale. There are two approaches to large-scale space planning. The first is to set your ideal space allocation, for example 50% collections, 30% readers, 15% staff and administration, and 5% service area. The other approach is to start with the quantities of volumes, readers, computers and such that you want to have in the space and see how much space is left for other functions. For example, if a library must contain shelving for 100,000 volumes, that amount of space is designated first and everything else must adapt. With a limited amount of space, this may result in less space than is wanted for other library functions. During the programming process you may decide to adjust your priorities in order to achieve an improved space allocation.

Once the large-scale decisions are at least tentatively made, the program plan moves to the small scale. The consultant should be able to recommend typical space requirements for a reader space or an office. If the consultant is familiar with libraries, she should be able to make recommendations about the number of volumes per square foot of collection space with your typical shelving dimensions, and for various types of work areas, such as that for a staff person processing books (who needs one or two book trucks next to the desk). However, it is best to double-check the consultant's recommendations by measuring for yourself the amount of space in your ideal reader spaces, computer workstations, and processing work spaces.

One resource for developing building projects for new public libraries or renovations is Libris Design software. It is a program to create building programs and cost estimates for construction, fixtures and furnishings. Users tailor generic models to their specific projects. The software operates on Microsoft Access and was developed by the California State Library.

The software is available to individuals who have taken a workshop in its use. The workshops are given in California, but arrangements can be made to have a workshop conducted locally. Information on the software and the workshops is available at www.Librisdesign.org. Also on the website are detailed essays on more than a dozen topics relating to facility planning including acoustics, lighting, furniture, shelving, and security.

SUMMARY PROGRAM • M. D. ANDERSON LIBRARY

DEPARTMENT • COMPONENT	DEPARTMENT TOTAL ASF	USER SEATS
• ENTRANCE and LOBBY	7,721	
• ACCESS SERVICES	29,278	
Service Point and Staff Workspaces	9,038	
User Spaces	11,000	276
Collections	9,240	
• INFORMATION SERVICES	11,001	
Service Point and Staff	4,921	
User Spaces	3,560	112
Collections	2,520	
• ELECTRONIC PUBLICATIONS CENTER	22,590	360
• GENERAL COLLECTIONS	133,474	
• MATERIALS USE	86,202	2,339

(additional areas have been deleted from this example)

PROGRAM • M. D. ANDERSON LIBRARY

DEPARTMENT • COMPONENT	QTY	ASF	Total ASF	DEPARTMENT TOTAL ASF	USER SEATS
ACCESS SERVICES User Spaces				**10,000**	**276**
• Patron/Staff Service					
• Lobby/Turnstiles/Security	1	200	200		
• User Stations and Seating					
• Display Area	1	200	200		
• Public Use Terminals	10	50	500		
• General Reader Seats (Tables)	110	30	3,300		110
• General Reader Seats (Carrels)	50	35	1,750		50
• General Reader Seats (Lounge)	50	25	1,250		50
• Microform Reader/Printer Stations	12	50	600		12
• Video Viewer Stations	30	50	1,500		30
• Collaborative Work Rooms w/ Tech (6 seats)	2	200	400		12
• Collaborative Work Rooms w/ Tech (12 seats)	1	300	300		12
ACCESS SERVICES Collections				**9,240**	**0**
• Collections by Type					
• Bound & Video: 31K Volumes, 150 DFS @ 210 vol each (90" high units)	150	18	2,700		
• File Cabinets for Reserve Materials	4	80	320		
• Current Journals Collections: 5,000 Titles, 60 Titles/DFS on display shelves = 110 DFS	110	22	2,420		
• Sorting Area	1	200	200		
• Open Microforms Cabinets: 200	200	18	3,600		

* Assignable Square Feet

At this stage in the planning you will continue to think of details that do not belong in the program plan, but that you do not want to lose track of. Continue to make notes about things that matter to you. If you are planning a large space, subdivide the notes by area. Does the wall of the reading room need to accommodate a donor portrait or a particular piece of art? Do you want space for a handout rack in the lobby? Does the lounge need plumbing for a coffee machine? As these ideas come to you and your colleagues, remember to capture them in a particular place, not buried in meeting notes.

Program planning is a time of trade-offs. You will almost certainly want more volumes, computers, and reader spaces than there is room for. Keep an eye on the goals you set early in the planning process. Revise them if necessary, but push back if the program begins to add nonessentials at the expense of core components.

The consultant or architect who assists with the program planning can often provide information on typical construction costs. If at this stage the library has some idea of a project budget, the program planning process can provide the first project budget reality check.

The design architect will take the program plan as a guideline, not a prescription. Your program plan showing a 500 square foot lobby may end up as a floor plan with 425 square feet or 600 square feet, depending on what is next to the lobby and how the pieces are fitted together. This is where your notes come into play in order to advise the architect that the lobby needs to accommodate not only the walk-off surface and access to the doors, but also the handout rack and room for 20 people to wait for it to quit raining.

PLANNING DOCUMENTS: ADJACENCY DIAGRAMS, FLOOR PLANS, 3-D VIEWS, AND ROOM DATA SHEETS

The program may include a goals statement, adjacency information, descriptions of room finishes, information about mechanical systems and the space they occupy, information about furnishings, and a description of the site. However, all of these may be contained in other documents instead.

Adjacency diagrams are typically next after the program plan. These may be presented as a matrix that looks like the "mileage between cities" chart on a road map (with, instead of miles at the junctions, a symbol indicating whether the intersecting spaces should be close to each other or not), or as a bubble diagram with the bubbles for, say, the checkout desk and the book collection either closer to each other or farther apart. In either case the building services are listed, and the goal is to put as close together the services that need to be close to one another, to separate the ones that should be separated, and arrange the rest as they should flow from one to another.

A typical adjacency matrix or diagram would show the location of the public entrance, then the services that are to be near the entrance (Does the user first see the information desk or the checkout desk?). Identify relationships throughout the space (What staff unit is closest to the loading dock? Where are the work areas of the public service staff in relation to the service desk? Does the user pass the main reading areas before getting to the book collection?). Finally, there will inevitably be compromises as everything cannot be in the ideal relationship to everything else.

	Entry	Circulation	Reference Service	Public Computers	Reading	Collections	Processing	Administration	Mail Receiving	Server Room	Mechanical Room
Entry											
Circulation	+										
Reference Service	+	+									
Public Computers	o	o	+								
Reading	o	o	o	o							
Collections	o	o	o	o	+						
Processing	o	o	o	o	o	o					
Administration	o	o	o	o	o	o	o				
Mail Receiving	o	o	o	o	o	o	+	o			
Server Room	o	o	o	o	o	o	o	+	o		
Mechanical Room	-	o	o	o	-	o	o	o	o	o	

The Adjacency Matrix isn't fancy, but it is easy to do, and easy to revise.
This example is for an academic library.

The Bubble Diagram is much more attractive, but it is much more laborious to change, and requires a bit of artistic ability to create. This example is for a public library.

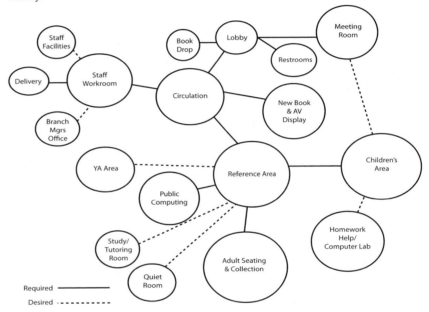

Required ———————
Desired ·-------------

Rendering

Photograph

The adjacency diagrams are then fitted into the envelope of the space (more compromises). Floor plans are next. This is the point at which the architect begins to visualize the interior spaces, but we library staffers who lack their turn of mind may not. There are several types of 3-D views that can help the planners communicate with us at this stage. The first is the 3-D line drawing used later in this publication. These views can be generated by the architect's CAD (Computer-Aided Design) software.

Another type of 3-D view is the **rendering**, which is a hand-drawn or computer-generated sketch of the space. Renderings can show the proposed colors and can be remarkably like the finished space.

Room data sheets are not used on all projects. They are recommended for smaller projects. Data sheets should be used in larger projects, for rooms that have special features. As the room data sheets are prepared, compare them with your notes and add the special features you thought of earlier. Architects typically consider room data sheets to be useful during design and construction, and discardable afterwards. However, if the room data sheets are kept up-to-date with changes made during construction they can provide a record of the type of carpet, brand and color of paint, which outlet is connected to which breaker, which walls are weight-bearing, and other

M.D. Anderson Library at University of Houston

useful information. Each architect or designer has their own format for room data sheets, and many examples can be found later in this text and in the books in the bibliography.

COMPLY WITH STANDARDS

If your planning is part of a construction project or a renovation, you need to ensure that someone involved with your project is designated to ensure that the appropriate code reviews are conducted. It is also not unusual for a construction project to include a life safety consultant and/or an ADA consultant. This area is complex because, even though there is a national Fire Code and ADA is a Federal law, there are state and local interpretations of each. Also, your project will be subject to a variety of codes. It is not unusual for architects, life safety consultants, fire marshals, and ADA officials to disagree. In the end, your local fire marshal and ADA official have the final authority to make decisions in their respective areas. Even if the architect disagrees, the decisions may unfortunately mean that the exact dimensions of your service desk may have to change, or the space you had intended for a reader table may become part of the path to a fire exit.

If, on the other hand, you are rearranging space or buying new furniture it is your responsibility to ensure that the appropriate administrator has these plans reviewed and approved. Your new furniture may need to be ADA compatible, and if you are rearranging furniture in an existing space, you may inadvertently violate a fire code. An example of the latter would be arranging a work space so that the route to the fire exit is too narrow or exceeds the maximum length allowed.

SPACE-THE BIG BLOCKS

As part of your planning process you will determine the amount of space needed for collections, readers, and staff. However, your building or space must also accommodate a number of areas that you as a newly-minted library planner may not think about or may not know how to calculate. For example, if the architect is talking about a 4,000 square foot space, not all of it will be yours. The unassignable area, circulation, and vestibule spaces described below all come "off the top."

ASSIGNABLE, UNASSIGNABLE AND GROSS AREA

The **assignable area**, also called the **programmable area**, or the **net area** (all of these mean the same thing) is the part that can be used for library and other discretionary functions. It includes most of the public space of the building. The assignable, or programmable, space is the major topic of this book. However we will detour for just a few sentences to explain the unassignable area.

The **unassignable area** is the portion of the building that supports the use of the building. The unassignable area can be divided into two parts. The first part of the unassignable area is used by the public and staff, and is deemed unassignable because it must be used for predetermined functions. These include stairs, elevators, restrooms, vestibule, and the main corridors that lead to exits and from one part of the building to another, whether or not these corridors are walled in as halls.

The second part of the unassignable area consists of: 1) the wall thicknesses, and 2) the spaces that the public never sees and that even the staff may seldom see—the mechanical, electrical and telecommunications rooms, the custodial closets, the spaces where the air vents and pipes go from floor to floor, or the little room containing the ladder to the roof.

The **gross area** is the total of the assignable and unassignable space.

In planning new construction the gross area is calculated by adding a percentage to the assignable space. The building is often budgeted and constructed to the size of the gross area. However, the initial calculation of assignable space is an estimate, and, as the actual stairs, air ducts, restrooms and such are included in the plan, the finished building may have a slightly higher or a slightly lower percentage of assignable space. (More assignable space is better. A building that maximizes assignable space is said to be "space efficient.")

The percentage of assignable to unassignable space varies with the size of the building. Smaller buildings are more space-efficient because they do not have as much space devoted to air ducts, stairwells, elevators, and required main corridors. The trade-off is that smaller buildings are usually more expensive per square foot to build (because they have proportionally more exterior wall) and are more expensive to operate (due to the loss of heating and cooling through the exterior walls and roof).

Building Blocks for Planning Functional Library Space

Here is the typical proportion between assignable and unassignable space in buildings of various sizes:

- Up to 40,000 square feet—75% of the space assignable, 25% unassignable (or, take the assignable and add 33.3%)
- 40,001-80,000 square feet—69% assignable, 31% unassignable (or, take the assignable and add 45%)
- Over 80,000 square feet—65% assignable, 35% unassignable (or, take the assignable and add 50%)

Note that these numbers are for whole buildings. If your library will occupy only part of a building your percentage of assignable space will probably be higher, because the central building service such as the fire water tank and main air conditioner room will not be in your space.

PLANNING THE ASSIGNABLE AREA
The text below is far from a complete guide. It hits only the high spots, plus a few quirks and details that the authors really want to highlight.

Circulation
Circulation space consists of aisles, halls, and other walking-around areas. Circulation space is unassignable, but you may be able to relocate an aisle to suit the design goals of your project. For example, the required walkway between the front door and the stairs may be able to be moved slightly to lead past the service desk. Also, a required circulation space may be capable of double duty, as when a required walkway to stairs, elevators, or exits can serve as the main walkway to a reading area or a collection space.

Note that discussions with architects and planners about "circulation space" in the Library's "Circulation service area" can become particularly confusing. For the purposes of planning discussions, consider calling your Circulation service "Checkout."

Vestibule and Transition
The vestibule is the entry into the library from outdoors, or from a very different area such as a mall. A vestibule may be as simple as the area for a door to swing. If the entry is from the outdoors, you will want a sufficient walk-off surface (such as a mat or grating) to keep most of the dirt, water, and debris from getting into your space.

The transition space consists of whatever you want people to see about your library as they walk past or enter. It can be as simple as a new book shelf or a sign inside the door, or as grand as the stone lions, steps, and grand concourse of the New York Public Library. In any case, this is the space that says "this is a library, not a . . ." (insert your favorite comparison), and says what kind of library it is—the sort with stone lions and vaulted ceilings, or technical books and journals, or leisure reading and homework help.

The transition space is also the place for good signage and, if possible, good sightlines to collections, services, and building amenities such as stairs and restrooms.

Collections

Library shelving constitutes the largest single allocation of space in a conventional library. Shelving installations are fraught with opportunities for mismeasurement and misunderstanding.

Most of the newer library shelving consists of a welded rectangular frame to which the base assembly and the book shelves are attached. One frame with its base and shelves is called a section. The width (also called the length) of the section is the measurement from one end of the frame to the other. A typical section of library shelving is 36" wide. However, this varies slightly by manufacturer, and some library shelving is as much as 36 1/2 " wide.

One section is bolted to the next to assemble a range. A range of shelving may also have an end panel on one or both ends. The end panel may be attached with a bracket. The width of the end panel and the bracket must be included in the measurement of the length of a range.

The depth of the shelving is the assembled depth of the base. The word "assembled" is important because the depth of shelving is not measured by the vendor in the way that you might expect. Manufacturers typically quote the *nominal* depth of a shelf, which is the actual depth plus the inch that the back of the book can hang over the back of the actual shelf into the space created by the depth of the frame. The upright part of the frame is typically 2" deep. So, if the shelving is assembled double-faced (with a shelf on each side), each actual 6" shelf can accommodate a book 7" deep.

The manufacturer may quote the depth of the base shelves in nominal or in actual inches. If the base comes in two parts that are bolted to each side of

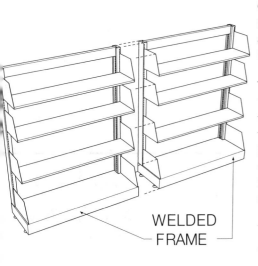

WELDED
FRAME

the frame, it is typically measured in the same way the shelf is measured, as a nominal depth. That is, if you buy a 10" base, the actual base will be only 9" deep. However, the double-faced bases from some manufacturers are a single piece that extends though the frame from one side to the other (forming two base shelves), and these are often measured by the vendor in actual ruler dimensions. If you are moving existing shelving, measure the depth before you take it apart. If you are buying new shelving, ask the vendor to send you the measurement of an assembled base.

The floor space required by a range of shelving is determined by a combination of the width (or length) of the range (measuring from end-to-end as you face the shelves), the depth of the widest part of the range from front to back (the widest part may be the base shelf, or it may be the end panel), and the aisles around the range. A range of shelving requires aisle space on all four sides. (Unless, of course, one side is installed against a wall.) ADA requires the aisles **between** ranges of shelving to be at least 36" wide and preferably 42". Some local jurisdictions require the 42" aisle width, which is more comfortable, particularly in public libraries. All of the aisles **around** a block of shelving (a rectangular group of ranges) must be at least as wide as the aisles between the ranges. However, if any of the aisles serve as passage spaces (to a fire exit or reader area), they may have to be wider than they would need to be for access to the book shelving alone. These passage aisles are typically required to be between 5 feet and 8 feet wide, with wider aisles being required in high-capacity buildings and higher-traffic areas.

The frame of older library shelving typically consists of four pieces bolted together to form the rectangular frame. With this type of shelving the uprights may come in two versions, a narrower one (intended to be installed at the end of the range of shelving) with only one column of slots to attach shelves, and a wider one (intended to be installed within the length of the range) that has two adjacent columns of slots to attach shelving. If you are rearranging shelving of this type, and making more ranges than you had originally, you may not have enough of the narrower uprights. You may be able to accommodate the extra width of these uprights in ranges where a section of shelving is deleted to fit around a column. If not, your plan will have to allow for some ranges that are an inch or so longer than the others.

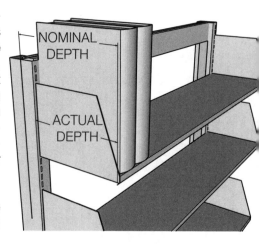

If you are re-using existing shelving, and you have any suspicion that the shelving was custom-made to fit the current space, it is best to measure all of it. Older libraries often contain shelving with non-standard dimensions.

Many library planners have been bitten by these complications, and if your architect or space planner is not familiar with libraries (and even if he is) this part is easy to get wrong. In the past these miscalculations often resulted in narrower than desired stack aisles. However, today in most jurisdictions ADA requires a 36" aisle width between ranges of shelving, and at least 36" between the last face of the shelving and any other wall or furniture. A miscalculation of the width of the assembled shelving can lead to installation of far less shelving than was expected.

User services
Do you plan to provide reference and information service at a massive desk that is part of the architectural statement? Or do you want to meet library users wherever they are conducting their tasks? Or do you want consultation rooms? If the space is flexible enough, it may accommodate several service models during its lifetime. However, the furniture and other fittings of the flexible space will probably not have the permanent, quality look of a built-in granite-topped desk.

Readers
Newer libraries often have more diversity in reader spaces than older libraries. The standard seat-at-a-table or at-a-carrel is often supplemented by lounge seating, adjustable-height seats for those who bring their own computers, and food service areas. Users want electrical outlets at their seats for their computers and also for their many other rechargeable devices.

Staff
At some point in the planning process you will probably be tempted to cut staff space in order to meet your own goals for public space. You may be tempted by the pull in the other direction, to increase staff space because "we have been working in poor conditions and we deserve better." Being the public-service-oriented profession that we are, we often shortchange ourselves. If your staff is processing materials for this building (and in the future also for remote storage) they may need more space, not less. As technology support becomes more complicated it may take more space, not less. If books go away you will not need book trucks in the processing area, but until that happens it is not reasonable for a person who processes books to work without one or two adjacent book trucks.

Technology

The older CRT computer monitors required deeper work surfaces than do the newer flat-panel monitors. If you are redesigning a computer area or buying new furniture for one, you may want to consider replacing the CRT monitors as part of the process. You will be able to use furniture that is shallower from front to back, and to thereby get more users into the same square footage without decreasing the space available to the user. However, the CPU part of the computer has not changed dimensions over time, and the small-cube models that are available are typically more expensive and less upgradable than the typical desktop or short-tower CPU cases.

Users will also want electrical outlets at the computer workstations to re-charge their cell phones and other devices. They may want to plug in their own laptop to transfer information.

Electrical outlets in public areas

More and more users come to the library with their own computers and ap-preciate wireless access. The "wireless" of course applies only to the data, not the power. These users will string power cables across walkways if there is no power outlet adjacent to the table or chair where they want to use the computer.

Although the next two topics are admittedly minor in the context of a con-struction plan, they are frequently overlooked opportunities to improve your design.

Building codes require a certain number of utility outlets, placed along the walls for use by custodians. Architects often do not discuss with owners the locations of these code-required utility outlets, but it is a good idea for you to raise the issue. Try to have the outlets placed where they will not be obstructed by shelving or furniture, but adjacent to seating or study tables where they can meet some of the public need. If the utility outlets are likely to be heavily used by your public, you can also request that fewer of these outlets be placed on each electrical circuit. This will make it less likely that the circuit breakers will be tripped.

Users with powered wheelchairs also need to recharge. Recharging a wheelchair can draw a lot of power, and can trip circuit breakers and disable any computers being used on the same circuit. If possible, designate some easy-to-reach outlets, each on a separate circuit, for wheelchair charging. Wheelchair-bound users often appreciate having these outlets adjacent to the ADA accessible computers.

USING THE DIAGRAMS TO PLAN YOUR SPACE

There are many ways to use the following drawings of library equipment and furnishings. The drawings may be useful at the program planning stage, to illustrate just how much square footage to allow for a work space or a reader seat in your particular library. However, the primary use of the drawings will be as cutouts that you can move around as you plan the arrangement of a space.

Please feel free to photocopy the illustrations that follow. If you reduce the images with a photocopier, check the scale of the copy—most copiers do not reduce a copy exactly by the dimension they are set to. You may need to set the reduction ratio to 49% or 52% to get a true half-size copy. One trick is to put a flat ruler on the glass of the copier, and copy the ruler beside the image. If you make a 50% copy, the 2" mark on the copied ruler should line up with the 1" mark on a real ruler.

As you cut out the desired furnishing from your copy, please include in your cutout not only the outline of the object but also the space that needs to be left free around it so it can be used—that is, after all, the most important point of this book.

A couple of good tricks are to use colored copy paper, and to stick a little bit of double-sided tape to the backs of your cutouts. You can tape down the furnishings more securely once you have the plan the way you want it, but it is better to be able to move the pieces fairly easily while you are revising the plan.

You may also want to use the illustrations as the basis for drawings of your unique furnishings. Use the illustrations as an indication of how much user space is needed for your unique furnishing.

Once you have the furnishings copied and cut out, to begin your plan, first obtain or draw a floor plan of the space. If you are planning an area larger than an individual office or work space you may prefer to use paper that has a lightly-printed grid. Most people prefer grids based on 1/8" or 1/4" per foot, rather than 1/10" or 1/5", because the latter grids do not help you divide a foot by one half or one quarter.

Next, if the area you are planning includes circulation space, show that on your plan.

Third, sketch on the plan or make notes at the side showing the flow of people or materials through the space. On your plan, do materials arrive from the mail room at the bottom of your sheet and exit on the right side? Do readers arrive on a stack floor from elevators to the left and stairs at the top of the page?

Now you are ready to lay out the furnishings on the plan. If you expect to make more than one version of your plan you can copy all of the furnishings that are to go into the space onto a single sheet of paper (or several sheets, if there are too many for one sheet), then cut out one set and arrange the space in one way. Start with a new blank floor plan and another sheet of furnishings for the next version. By putting all of the furnishings on a sheet you will reduce the need to count them repeatedly, and you will be more likely to include everything.

Introduction to Illlustrations

All the drawings on the following pages show both the plan and a three dimensional view of the furniture and equipment being illustrated. The dimensions given indicate the minimal requirements for clearance around each item. Where further considerations are needed, they are noted. In areas where rooms are described, there are examples of each room.

List of Illustrations

Public Areas

Illustrations, continued

Collection Areas

Item	Square Feet	Page Number
Atlas/Dictionary/Folio Stand	37.5 SF	**56**
Shelving (see Shelving sections for explanation)		**57**
Compact 10" base, single faced		
Media (15" base)	33 SF	
Periodical (15" base)	13 SF	
36" Aisle Width	240 SF	**59**
Base Shelf 10"	15 SF	
Base Shelf 12"	15.5 SF	
Base Shelf 15"	17 SF	
Base Shelf 18"	18.5 SF	
42" Aisle Width		**63**
Base Shelf 10"	16 SF	
Base Shelf 12"	17 SF	
Base Shelf 15"	18.5 SF	
Base Shelf 18"	20 SF	
48" Aisle Width		**67**
Base Shelf 10"	17.5 SF	
Base Shelf 12"	18.5 SF	
Base Shelf 15"	20 SF	
Base Shelf 18"	21.5 SF	
Compact Double - Faced Shelf	8 SF	**71**
Spinners	50 SF	**72**
(for paperbacks, CDs, CD-ROMS, cassettes)		
File Cabinets		**73**
Lateral	15 SF	
Vertical	7.5 SF	
Flat File/Map Case	23 SF	**75**
Audio Station	24 SF	**76**
Microform Cabinet - single faced	10.5 SF	**76**

Illustrations, continued

Reading/Study Areas

Item	Square Feet	Page Number
Study Area		**79**
Individual	23 SF	
Study Carrel	22 SF	
Enclosed - Individual study room	37.5 SF	
Chairs/Seats		**83**
Bench (freestanding)	23 SF	
Lounge Chair	121 SF	
Meeting Room Chair	10 SF	
Sofa - 2 person	30 SF	
Sofa - 3 person	48 SF	
Computer Workstations		**88**
Patron Access Computer	24 SF	
Group Study Room	150 SF	
Graphic Workstations (scanner, dual screen)	62 SF	
Tables		**91**
Two-seat (nose to nose) Adult	66 SF	
Four-seat - Adult	120 SF	
Six-seat - Adult	140 SF	
Booth Seating	48 SF	

Illustrations, continued

Illustrations, continued

Offices

Item	Square Feet	Page Number
Director		**116**
(including desk, credenza, guest seating, bookcases)	300 SF	
Staff Office - Large	200 SF	**117**
Staff Office - Medium	150 SF	**118**
Staff Office - Small	100 SF	**119**
Reception Area	150 SF	**120**
Supervisor Workstation	120 SF	**121**
Working/Sorting		
Equipment Repair Room	120 SF	**124**
Supply Room	150 SF	**125**
Recycling Containers	20 SF	**126**
Safe	11 SF	**127**
Book trucks	4.5 SF	**128**
Flat trucks	12 SF	**129**
Hand truck	3 SF	**130**
Mail Delivery Cart	5 SF	**131**
Supply/Storage Unit	14 SF	**132**
Vending Machine	19 SF	**133**

Public Areas

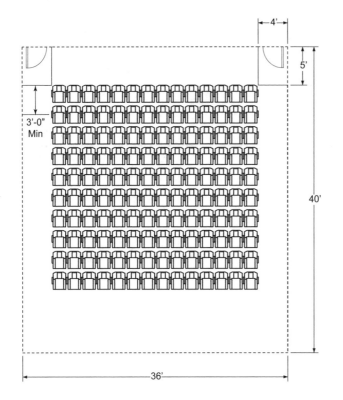

South Plainfield Public Library, Michigan.
Used by the permission of PSA-Dewberry

The diagram shown is for an auditorium containing 130 seats.

If a row extends for more than 13 seats, provide a greater back-to-back distance to allow for passage. The minimum back to back is 3' - 0".

Each auditorium should provide for a proportionate number of handicapped accessible seats. Refer to your local code or ADA guidelines.

If a stage or podium is desired at the front of the auditorium space, provide additional square footage in your program.

The stage or any raised platform must be handicapped accessible.

Provide access to storage, a stage, control room, etc. as needed.

Many auditoriums will require a sound or light lock at each entry point.

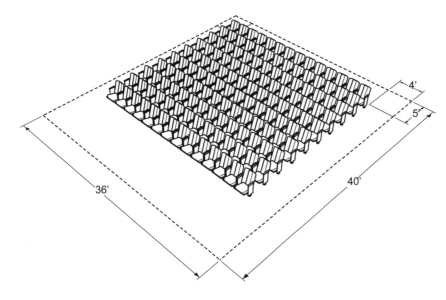

Auditorium Seating

1440 SF

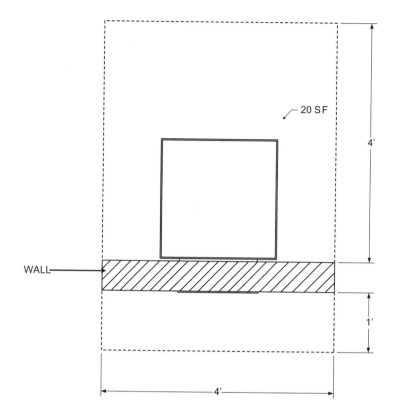

20 SF

4'

WALL

1'

4'

Used by the permission of Demco, Inc.

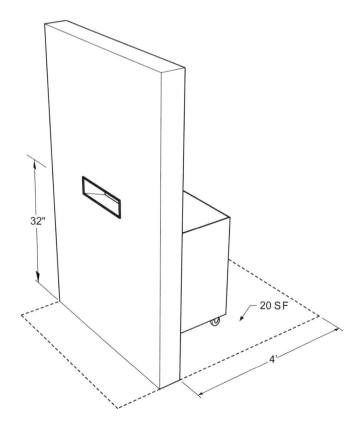

32"

20 SF

4'

The size of the book bin will affect the square footage needed.

The use of RFID sorting and layout will affect the square footage needs.

Provide a shelf or ledge for materials sorting in close proximity to the book drop.

The workspace of the check-in side needs to accommodate the work flow, keeping checked in and unchecked materials separated and allowing space for items that need to be put aside for mending or other attention. This space also needs to accommodate any other requirements (such as electricity, data cable connections, or shielding) of any check-in equipment such as scanning terminal or RFID equipment.

The slot opening should allow for the return of oversized books without allowing the people to reach into the bin.

Local fire codes may require that the book drop room be a separate room with fire rated walls.

Book Drop - External thru-wall

20 SF

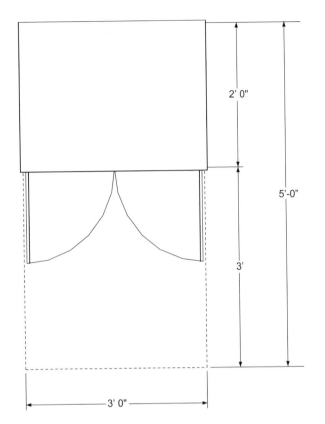

Provide space for opening doors and maneuvering the book bin in the adjacent area.

Consider if side-by-side return bins are required for both print materials and AV materials.

To limit damage to returned materials, the interior of the bin should be padded or depress as it is filled.

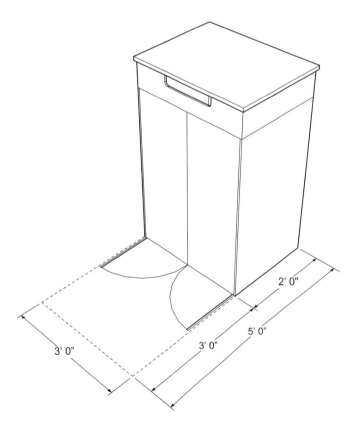

Book Drop - Internal Free Standing   15 SF

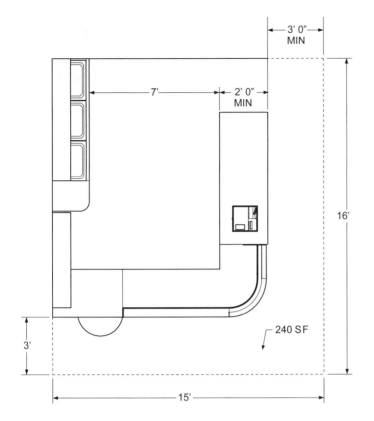

Firewheel Church, Garland Texas.
Used by the permission of PSA-Dewberry

The local health department will dictate much of the design requirements. It is very important to review the layout and equipment requirements with local officials in early planning.

Plan early, and consider meeting with vendors about typical requirements needed to run the shop if considerations are made for soliciting vendors.

Most in-library cafés are operated by an outside vendor. Consult the vendor for specific requirements.

The sink is sometimes put into an adjacent storage closet. Some jurisdictions will require an ADA accessible sink with kneewell.

A triple sink is generally required to meet code and vendor requirements.

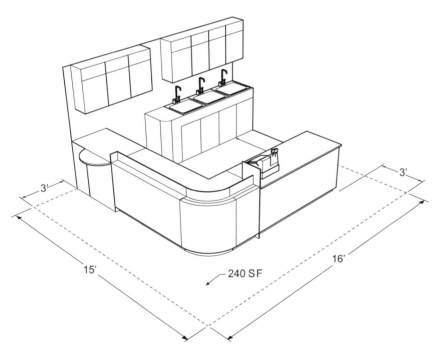

Café Counter   240 SF

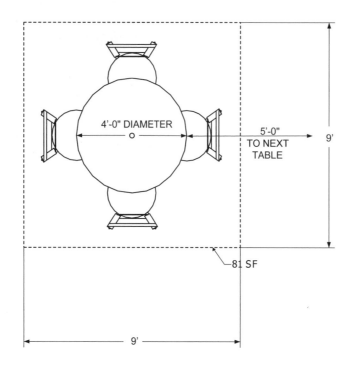

4'-0" DIAMETER

5'-0"
TO NEXT
TABLE

9'

81 SF

9'

Used by the permission of Demco, Inc.

Provide a mixture of seating types.

There are typically three heights of café tables available: 29", 36", and 42".

Make sure chair and table heights are coordinated.

When laying out multiples of café tables, provide five feet minimum clearance from table edge to table edge.

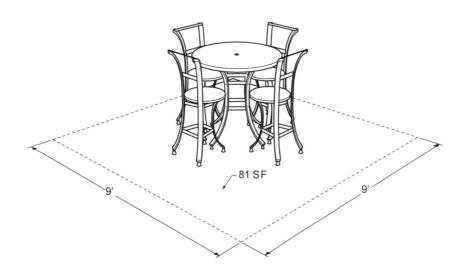

81 SF

9'

9'

Café Seating

81 SF

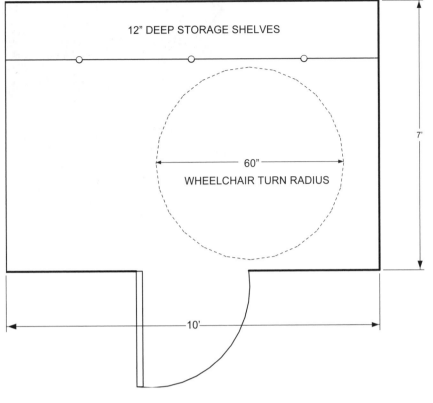

12" DEEP STORAGE SHELVES

60"
WHEELCHAIR TURN RADIUS

7'

10'

Typical Shelf Unit For Storage Room.
Used by the permission of H3 Hardy Collaboration
Architecture

All storage rooms must meet ADA guidelines for accessibility.

Many vendors require a locked storage closet in order for them to operate in your library.

This is another area, along with the café that must be coordinated with a vendor and with the local health department.

The café storage area might contain a sink.

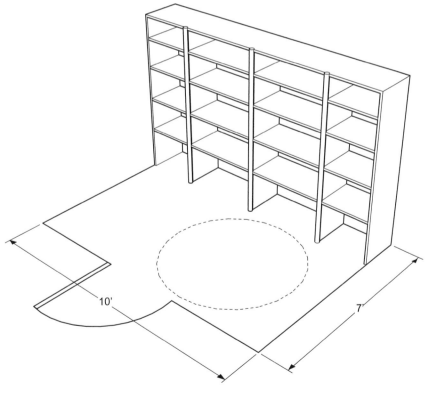

10'

7'

Café Storage

70 SF

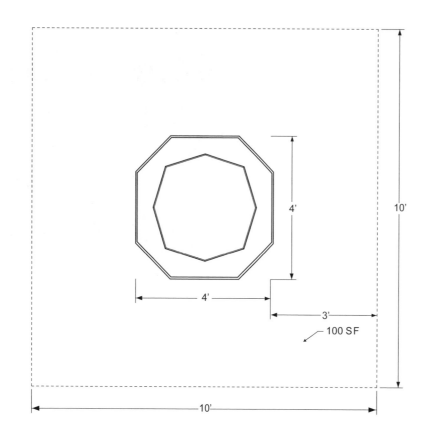

Jacksonville Public Library, San Marcos
Used by the permission of AGATI Furniture

There are many types and sizes of display units to choose from.

Open, accessible units encourage browsing.

Plan for the display unit's size plus a minimum 3' perimeter clearance to the next object.

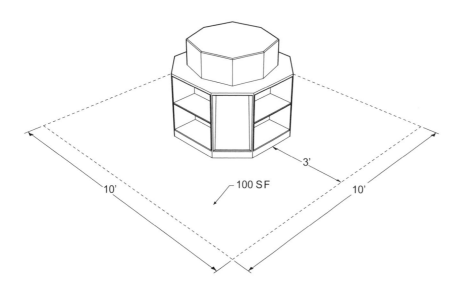

Display - Free Standing Book Display   100 SF

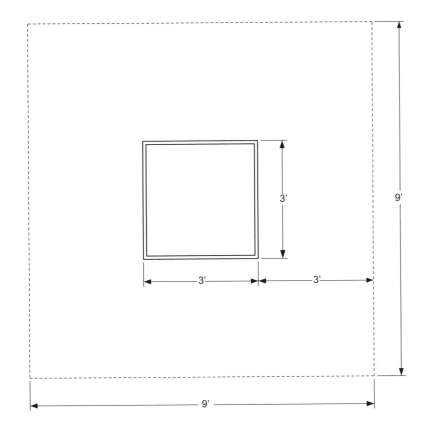

Chicago Botanical Garden
Used by the permission of AGATI Furniture

There are many types and sizes of display cases to choose from.

Enclosed display cases provide a high level of security for items on display.

Display cases can also provide temperature and humidity control for fragile items.

Provide access to power outlets proximate to display cases for lighting.

Plan for display unit's size plus minimum 3' perimeter clearance to the next object.

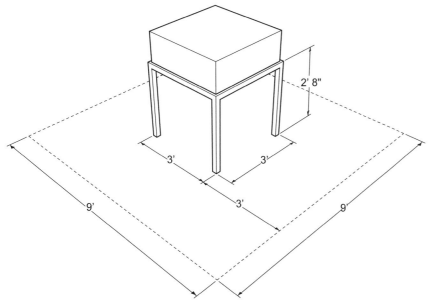

Display - Free Standing Display Case   81 SF

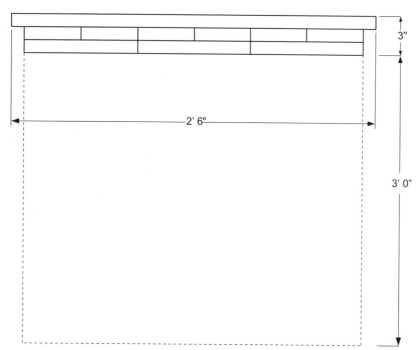

3"

2' 6"

3' 0"

Used by the permission of Demco, Inc.

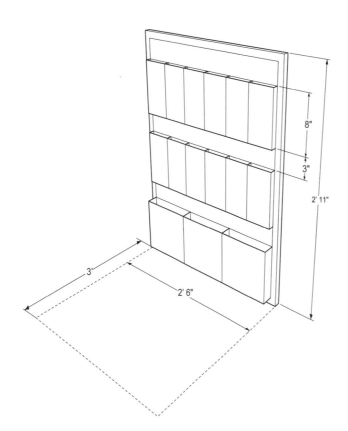

8"

3"

2' 11"

3'

2' 6"

Literature kiosks must be mounted to meet ADA access guidelines for heights and protrusions.

A variety of types and styles are available for display of community and library literature.

Lengths and depths of literature kiosks will vary.

Consider providing a variety of slot sizes to accommodate both newspapers and smaller sized handouts.

Provide a minimum of 3' clearance in front of all kiosks.

Display - Literature Kiosk - wall mounted

10 to 20 SF

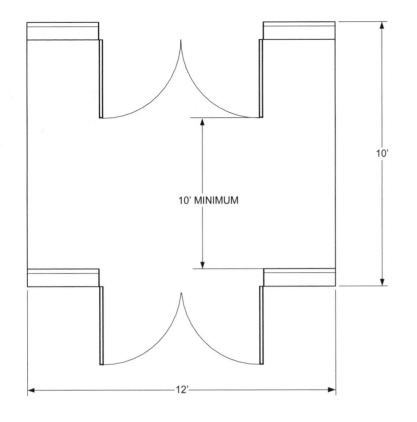

10' MINIMUM

10'

12'

Rockwall County Library, Texas
Used by the permission of PSA-Dewberry

Ideally, doors are located to allow one set to close before the second set opens.

Entry doors can be swinging or automatic sliding types.

Provide clear door space for doors to swing open.

If the entry is from outdoors, add a mat or other walkoff surface, preferably at least ten feet deep, to catch dirt, water and debris.

A grated walkoff surface may require less maintenance than mats, and is part of the construction of the building.

ADA allows for a minimum clearance of 10' between doors.

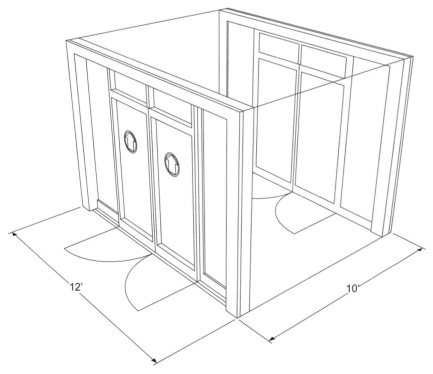

12'

10'

Entry Vestibule

120 SF

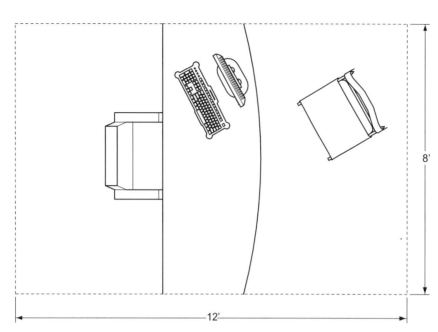

8'

12'

Rockwall Public Library, Texas
Used by the permission of PSA-Dewberry

The guest services desk should be placed in an easy to locate area on a major circulation path.

If providing a seated height desk, provide seating on both the patron and staff sides.

If the desk is standing height, an ADA height section is also required. This section is to be no higher than 34".

Guest services desk can be a seated or standing height desk. Some libraries use standing height greeter kiosk stations with seating of appropriate height on the staff side only. For increased flexibility greeter kiosk stations may be on wheels to be repositioned as needed.

Provide an area to fill out forms at a comfortable height.

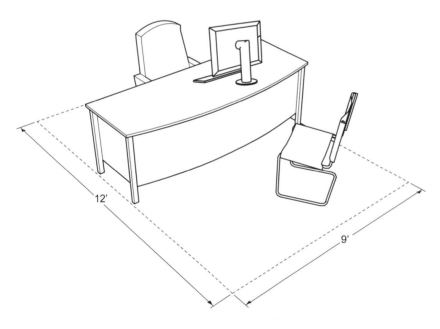

12'

9'

Guest Services Desk

96 SF

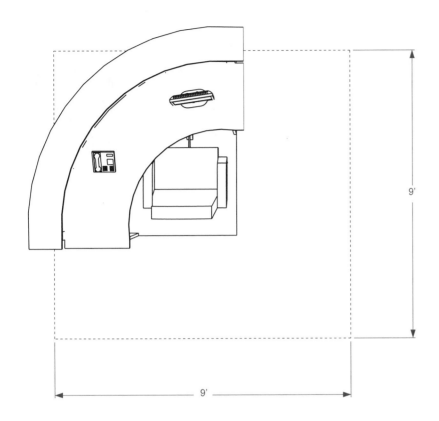

Greeter stations should be placed in a direct line of sight with the front entrance.

Greeter stations may be a variety of shapes and configurations.

Greeter stations are used to distribute directional information and program locations, but are not reference points.

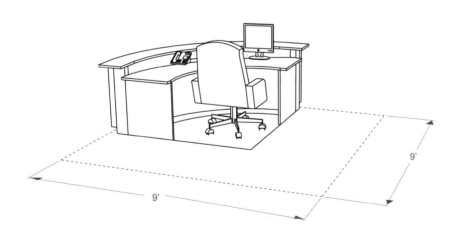

Greeter Station

81 SF

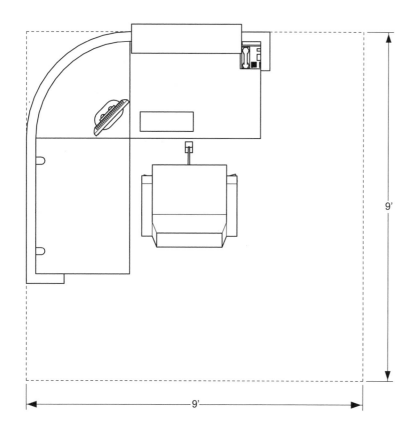

9'

9'

William T. Young Library at the University
of Kentucky, Lexington, KY
Used by the permission of Mary McLaren

Place the guard station in proximity to the entry doors, the book detection system and the circulation desk.

If security scanners are desired, add square footage as necessary.

If a sign-in area is required, provide writing height surface.

If a magnetometer and x-ray machine is required, provide these adjacent to the guard station. The square footage requirements for this items are approximately 80 square feet.

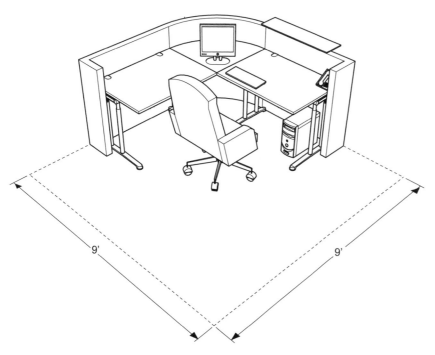

9'

9'

Guard Station

81 SF

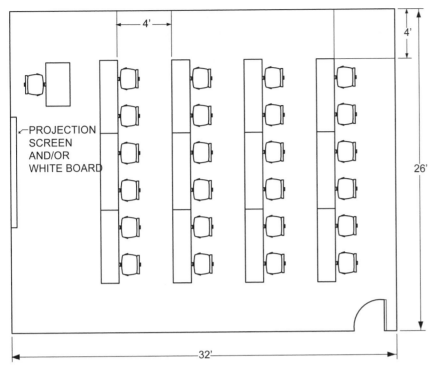

Columbia Public Library, Missouri
Used by the permission of Tom Kessler

Tom Kessler

Schaumburg Township Public Library, Illinois
Used by the permission of PSA-Dewberry

Hedrich Blessing

Provide a minimum of 3 square feet of surface for each desired occupant.

This room should be designed to provide flexibility in its configuration.

Provide for a variety of AV, power and data connections.

A percentage of seating must meet ADA guidelines for accessibility.

The depth of the work surface may be as little as 24", or even 22". Shallower work surfaces allow participants to be closer to the presenter.

Flat screen panels are sometimes preferred to projection screens. A flat screen panel replaces both the projector and screen.

White boards are sometimes supplemented or replaced by a "smart board" that captures the board contents.

PROJECTION SCREEN AND/OR WHITE BOARD

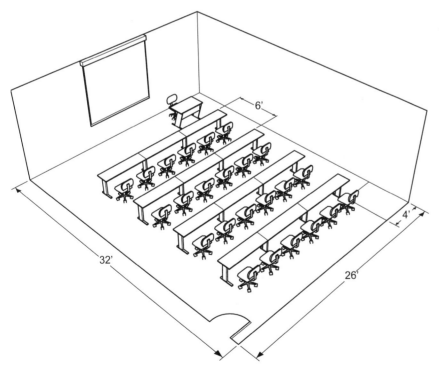

Classroom / Multipurpose Room

832 SF

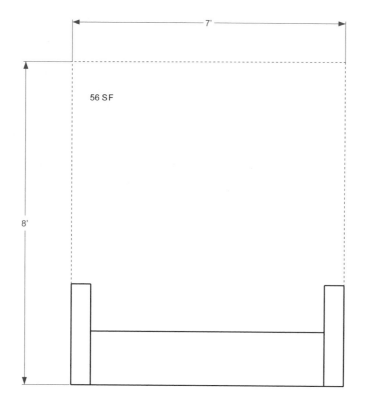

56 SF

Used by the permission of Demco, Inc.

Locate coat racks or coat closets so that they are visible to patrons.

Provide 4 inches for each coat to be accommodated.

To meet ADA requirements, some states require access to a lower level hanging coat bar.

Lengths of racks will vary, but generally the depth is 24".

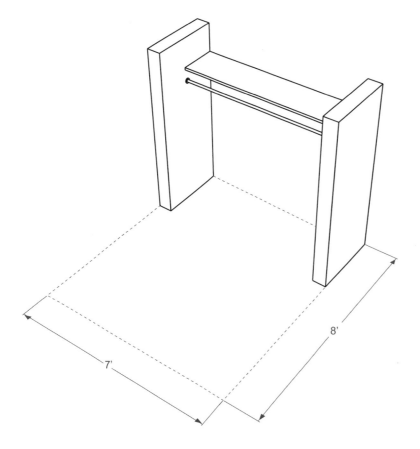

Coat Rack

56 SF

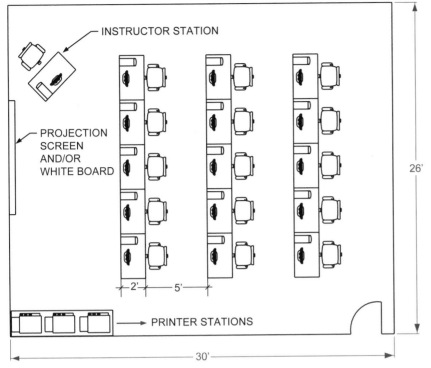

INSTRUCTOR STATION

PROJECTION SCREEN AND/OR WHITE BOARD

PRINTER STATIONS

2'   5'

30'

26'

Southfield Public Library, Michigan
Used by the permission of PSA-Dewberry

Traditional computer stations require a 42" x 24" deep work surface to house the computer screen.

Laptop computers require a minimum 36" x 24" deep work surface.

Provide tabletop or under table space to house CPU's.

This room should be designed to provide flexibility in its configuration.

Provide for a variety of AV, power and data connections.

Provide space for printers to be located.

Providing 5 feet from table edge to table edge will allow the instructor to walk behind the seated students.

Flat screen panels are sometimes preferred to projection screens. A flat screen panel replaces both the projector and screen.

White boards are sometimes supplemented or replaced by a "smart board" that captures the board contents.

30'

26'

Computer Classroom

780 SF

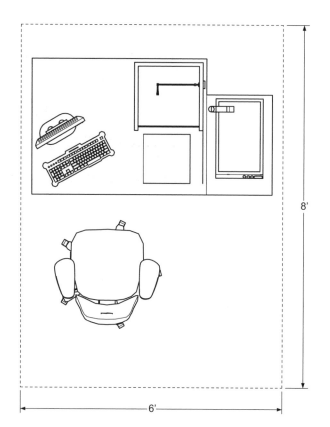

University of Houston
Used by the permission of Diane Bruxvoort

Design the desk to accept changing technology. Make it flexible and adaptable.

Determine whether this desk should be a sit-down or stand-up model.

The mobility and visibility of the desk should be considered.

Provide for connections to power and data outlets from this desk.

If a stand-up desk is utilized, it must be adjustable to meet ADA guidelines.

Equipment to consider with an instructor's desk or podium include a computer with monitor, DVD/VCR player, document camera, microphone/speakers, webcam and/or room camera for capturing presentation, space for laptop, and accessible USB ports and power supply.

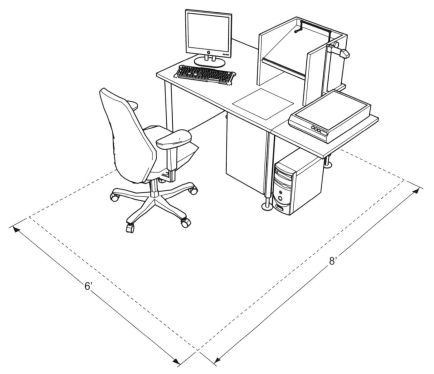

Computer Classroom - Instructor's Desk   48 SF

CREDENZA

5'

30'

15'

Orbitz Conference Room, Chicago Illinois
Used by the permission of AGATI Furniture

As a general guideline, provide a minimum of 25 square feet for each seat needed.

Provide space to circulate around the table. As a general rule, use 5' from the table edge to the wall if you are using a task chair. More space may be needed if you decide to use a larger executive chair. The size of the chair used at the table will have an impact on the amount of circulation space needed.

When determining the size of the conference room, consider the needs for AV and video conferencing equipment. Consider providing a credenza, near the door, for coffee service, supply storage and AV equipment storage.

If additional seating is required, you can place it against the far wall, but add 36" to the depth of the room.

Flat screen panels are sometimes preferred to projection screens. A flat screen panel replaces both the projector and screen but requires a computer.

White boards are sometimes supplemented or replaced by a "smart board" that captures the board contents.

Provide electrical outlets and data plugs for portable computers and AV equipment.

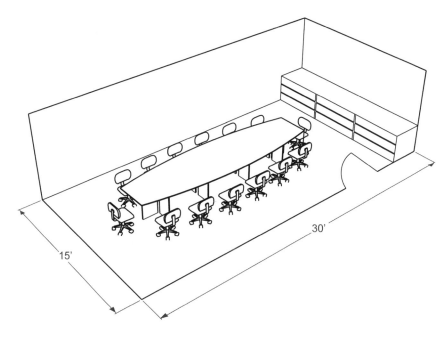

30'

15'

Conference / Board Room / Meeting Room   450 SF

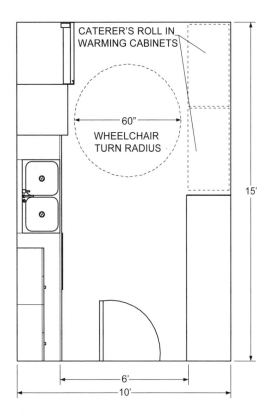

CATERER'S ROLL IN
WARMING CABINETS

60"

WHEELCHAIR
TURN RADIUS

15'

6'

10'

Used by the permission of H3 Hardy Collaboration Architecture

The minimum requirements for a catering kitchen include space for a refrigerator, microwave oven, sink and counter top. Caterers can always use blank space with outlets for when they roll in huge racks with their supplies.

Consider all appliances, including a dishwasher, ice maker and large freezer.

If a cook top is provided, it must be ventilated as per local code.

Standard base cabinets are 24 inches deep and require a minimum of 36 inches clear to a parallel surface or wall. Plan for adequate counter layout space.

Determine if a serving counter is desired, or if a pass thru to an adjoining room is needed.

The area under the sink must be handicapped adaptable, usually requiring removable base cabinets, in order to accommodate a wheelchair user.

Consider your need for an ice machine. Also consider adding a 22 volt outlet to support catering equipment.

Depth of sink should facilitate filling of large coffee urns. Consider providing a faucet with a flexible hose for filling purposes.

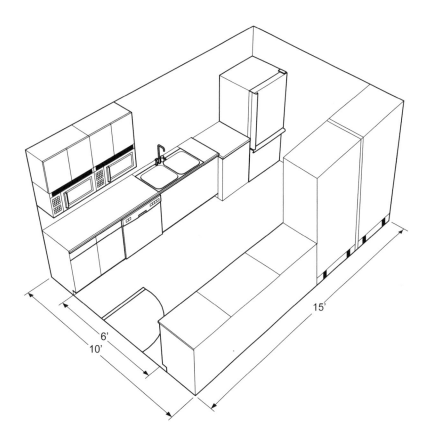

15'

6'

10'

Catering Kitchen

150 SF

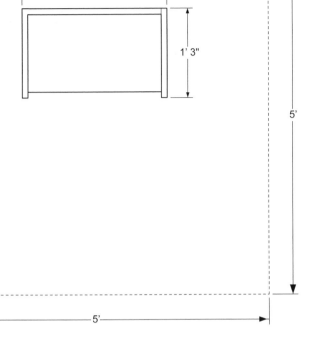

University of Houston
Used by the permission of Diane Bruxvoort

There are many types and styles of prefabricated podium/lectern units available for purchase.

Determine whether the podium or lectern should be a mobile or fixed unit.

Provide access to power and data outlets in close proximity to the podium/lectern.

Consider if an AV rack needs to be incorporated into the podium design.

Provide alternate presentation tables that meet ADA guidelines and accommodate seated individuals.

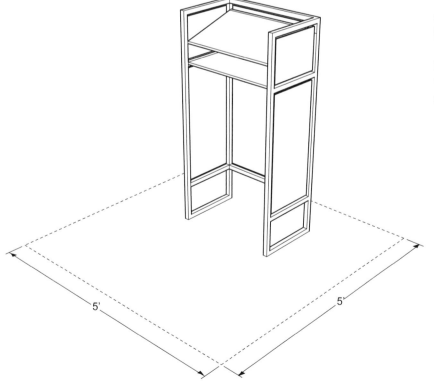

Podium / Lectern

25 SF

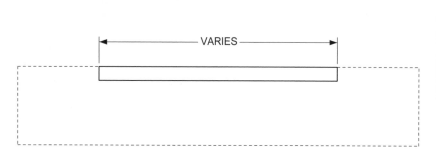

VARIES

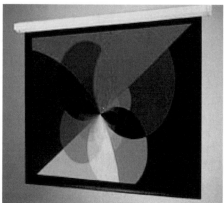

Projection screens can be ceiling hung, wall mounted or portable units.

Projection screens can be fixed, manually or electrically operated. If electrically operated, coordinate location of the controls with other AV elements of the room.

The size of the screen is determined by the room size and the location of the projector.

Rooms with projection capabilities tend to need additional square footage to accommodate a variety of seating and table layouts depending on the audience. Childrens room where children sit on the floor require larger square footages.

Flat screen panels are sometimes preferred to projection screens. A flat screen panel replaces both the projector and screen.

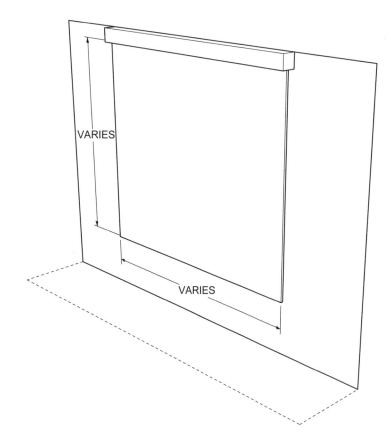

VARIES

VARIES

Projection Screen

No SF Needed

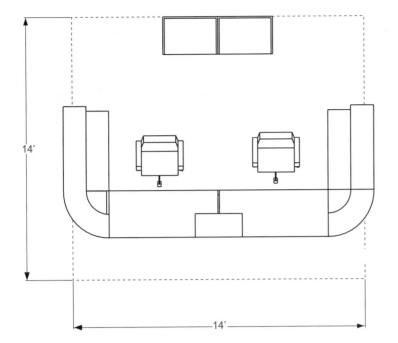

Dublin Public Library, Dublin California
Used by the permission of AGATI Furniture

The reference desk should be designed to offer flexible reconfiguration should your service model change.

Determine whether your desk should be a sit down or stand up service point.

If your staff person is seated, consider placing guest chairs at the desk for patron usage.

When planning your reference desk, consider the size needed to offer ample sight lines.

Plan the reference desk so that staff can easily exit from the unit.

Provide shelving space for reference material.

Provide space for adjacent book truck parking.

Provide ADA accessibility for both patrons and staff.

The height of the chairs at the desk needs to be adjustable. A good ergonomic chair will have an adjustable seat and back. Different staffers should be able to quickly and easily adjust chairs as they arrive at the desk.

As a rule of thumb typical heights for reference and circulation desks are as follows:
Standing Height Counter- 42" (range 39"-42")
Seating Height Counter- 32" (range 30"-34")
ADA compliant counter height- 34" maximum (verify with your local ADA code requirements)

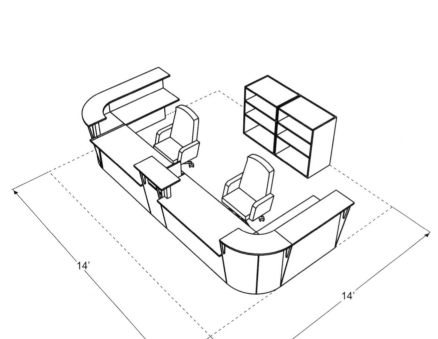

Reference / Information Desk

196 SF

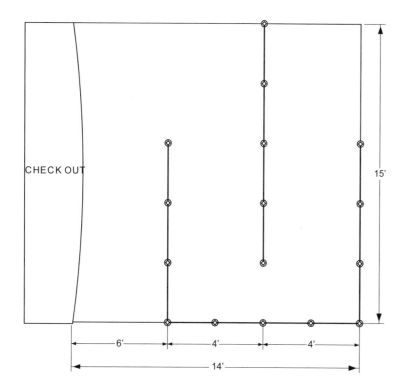

Schaumburg Township Public Library, Illinois
Used by the permission of PSA-Dewberry

Provide an adequate area for patrons waiting for service desk assistance or for self check out.

The queuing area can be designated by markings on the floor, railings or display elements.

The amount of queuing needed depends on the peak number of patrons served.

There are two basic types of queuing – multiple line and single line.

This illustration is for single line use.

Stanchions can be movable. A cover plate can be provided to insert into the hole if movable.

As a rule of thumb provide 3 SF per person for a queuing line at a circulation desk. You can also use 2-3 linear feet per person.

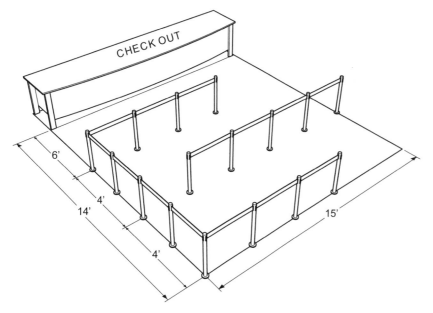

Queuing Area

210 SF

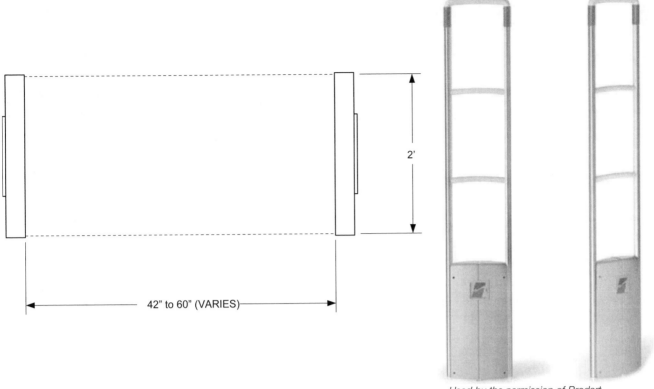

2'

42" to 60" (VARIES)

Spacing and location restrictions of security gates vary by manufacturer. A larger opening may require additional gates.

Carefully work with the security manufacturer on space and special requirements, as some gates can not be placed in proximity to metal objects.

Some security gates require electricity which requires consideration for the placement of conduits.

Avoid placing security gates in areas where book trucks tend to linger since books contain security strips that may set off the gates.

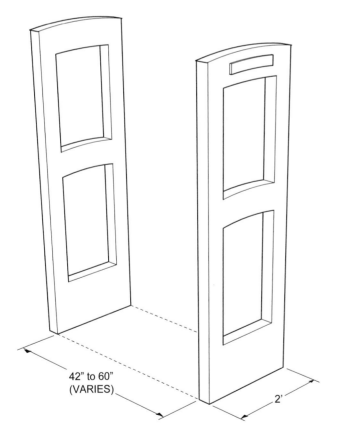

42" to 60" (VARIES)

2'

Security Gate

8 TO 10 SF

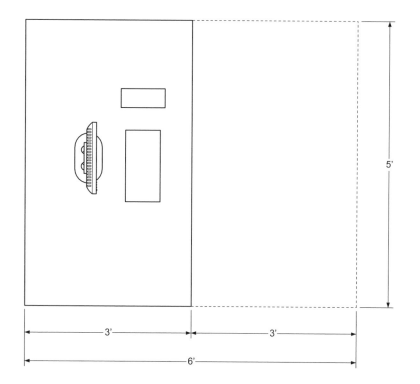

Self check size and shape will vary by manufacturer.

Many self checks are available with their own stand.

Custom stands can be constructed to meet specific needs.

Provide space on either side of the scanner unit to place library materials, purses, bookbags, etc.

The self check machine should be at an elevation and with adequate knee wall clearance to meet ADA guidelines.

Provide for a minimum of 36" clearance for a patron to stand while using the self check machine.

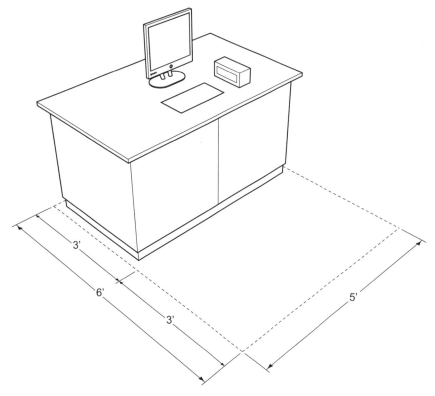

Self Check Machine

30 SF

Collection Areas

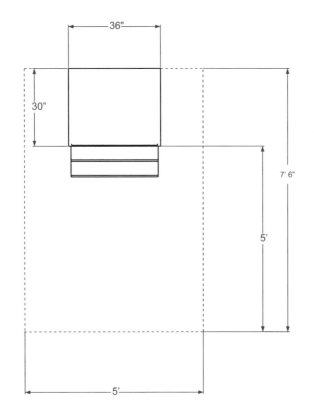

Menomonee Falls Public Library
Menomonee Falls Wisconsin
Used by the permission of AGATI Furniture

Provide access space for roll out shelves.

Provide for a minimum of 60" front clearance for a patron to stand while utilizing the atlas stand.

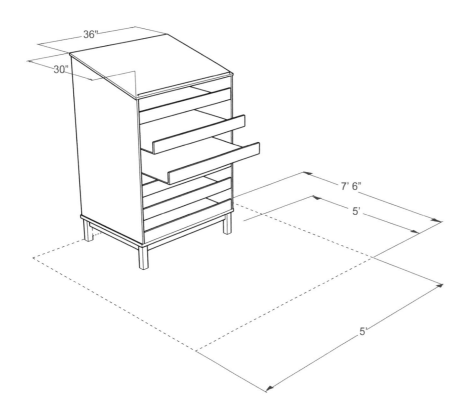

Atlas / Dictionary / Folio Stand

37.5 SF

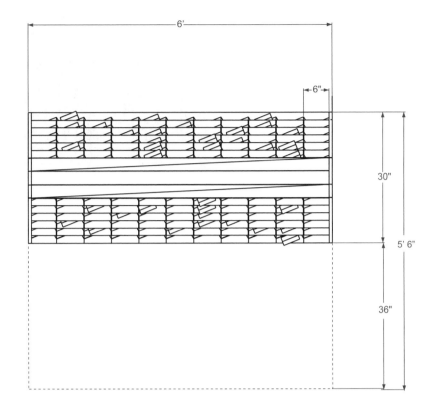

Tuckahoe Regional Library

Media shelving comes in a variety of sizes and styles. Different manufacturers have different sized footprints.

Single faced units should be secured to an adjacent wall to prevent overturning.

Allow for a minimum of 36" aisle widths between units or more if local accessibility guidelines require it.

Larger aisle widths will improve visibility of materials stored on lower shelves.

The type of shelf can vary with the type of media being shelved.

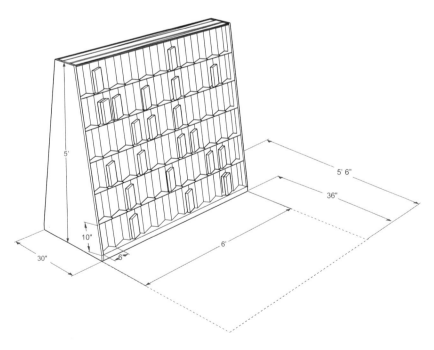

Shelving - Media

33 SF

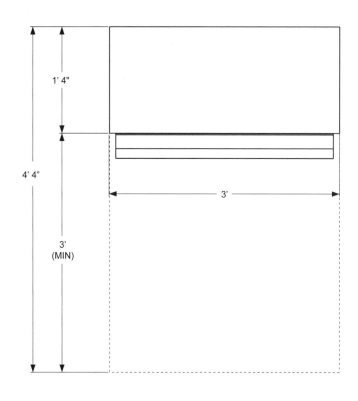

Used by the permission of Demco, Inc.

Periodical shelving comes in a variety of heights, usually 3, 4 or 5 shelves high.

Provide a minimum of 36" clearance in front of each wall mounted unit.

Single faced units should be secured to an adjacent wall to prevent overturning.

ADA restricts the height of current periodical shelving to a maximum of 54."

Consider shelving for back issues in another area. Back issues may also be housed in boxes.

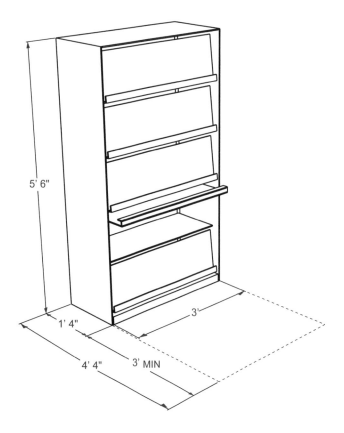

Shelving - Periodical

13 SF

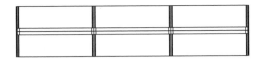

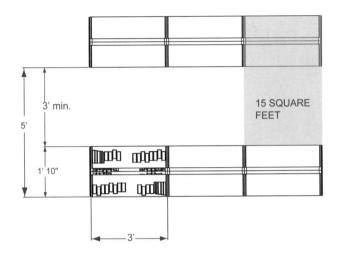

15 SQUARE
FEET

3' min.

5'

1' 10"

3'

If utilizing end panels, provide for 2 additional inches at the end of each range.

ADA presently allows a minimum of 36" aisles; however, 42" aisles are recommended.

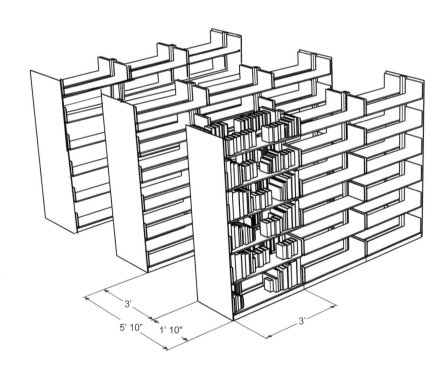

3'

5' 10"   1' 10"

3'

Shelving - 36" Aisle - Base Shelf 10"   15 SF

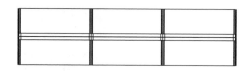

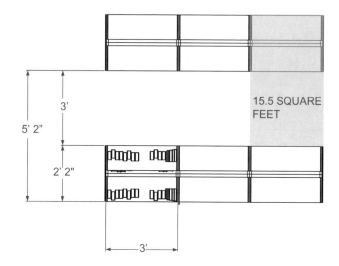

15.5 SQUARE FEET

5' 2"

3'

2' 2"

3'

Naperville Public Library, Naperville Florida
Used by the permission of AGATI Furniture

If utilizing end panels, provide for 2 additional inches at the end of each range.

Provide wider access aisle if top of low adjacent shelf unit is being utilized as a reference counter.

ADA presently allows a minimum of 36" aisles; however, 42" aisles are recommended.

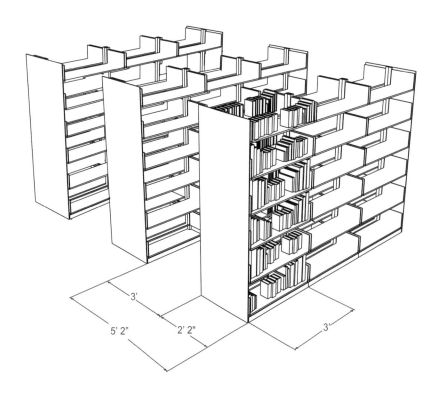

5' 2"   2' 2"   3'   3'

Shelving - 36" Aisle - Base Shelf 12"

15.5 SF

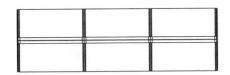

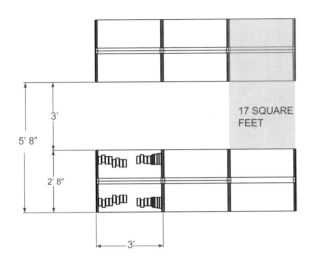

17 SQUARE
FEET

5' 8"

3'

2' 8"

3'

Naperville Public Library, Naperville Florida
Used by the permission of AGATI Furniture

15" base shelves are mainly utilized for magazines and display shelving.

If utilizing end panels, provide for 2 additional inches at the end of each range.

Provide wider access aisle if top of low adjacent shelf unit is being utilized as a reference counter.

ADA presently allows a minimum of 36" aisles; however, 42" aisles are recommended.

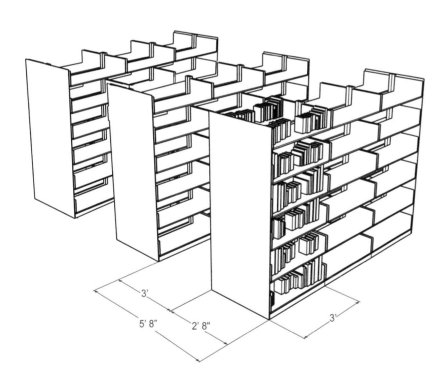

3'

5' 8"   2' 8"   3'

Shelving - 36" Aisle - Base Shelf 15"   17 SF

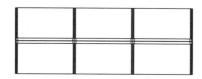

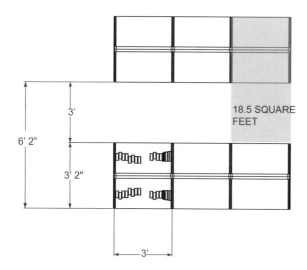

3'

6' 2"

3' 2"

18.5 SQUARE FEET

3'

18" base shelves are mainly utilized for shelving oversized and folio type materials.

If utilizing end panels, provide for 2 additional inches at the end of each range.

Provide wider access aisle if top of low adjacent shelf unit is being utilized as a reference counter.

ADA presently allows a minimum of 36" aisles; however, 42" aisles are recommended.

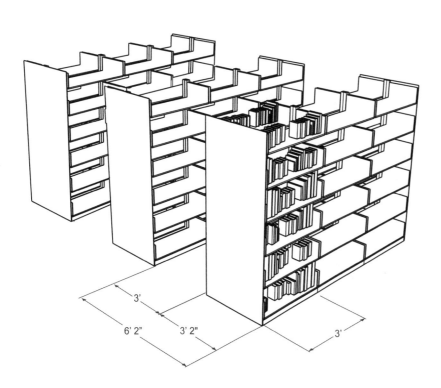

3'

6' 2"   3' 2"

3'

Shelving - 36" Aisle - Base Shelf 18"

18.5 SF

Albany Molecular Research Library
Used by the permission of Brodart Co.

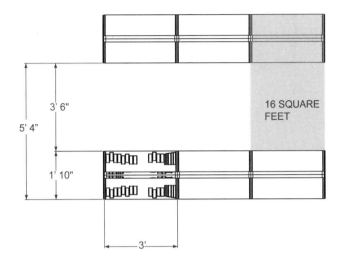

3' 6"

5' 4"

1' 10"

16 SQUARE FEET

3'

If utilizing end panels, provide for 2 additional inches at the end of each range.

Provide wider access aisle if top of low adjacent shelf unit is being utilized as a reference counter.

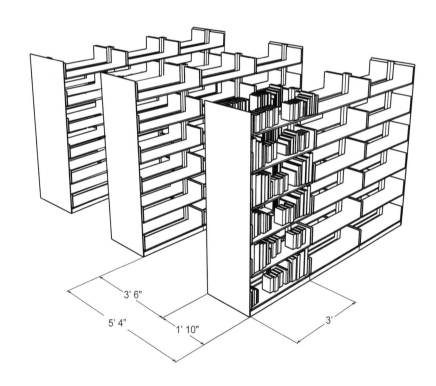

3' 6"

5' 4"

1' 10"

3'

Shelving - 42" Aisle - Base Shelf 10"

16 SF

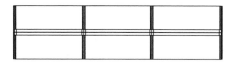

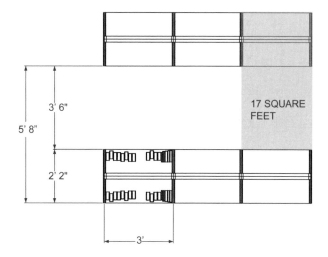

3' 6"

5' 8"

2' 2"

17 SQUARE FEET

3'

If utilizing end panels, provide for 2 additional inches at the end of each range.

Provide wider access aisle if top of low adjacent shelf unit is being utilized as a reference counter.

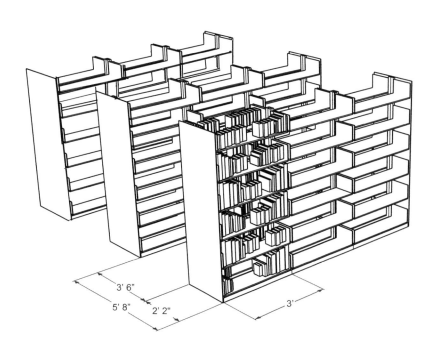

3' 6"

5' 8"   2' 2"   3'

Shelving - 42" Aisle - Base Shelf 12"   17 SF

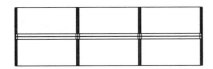

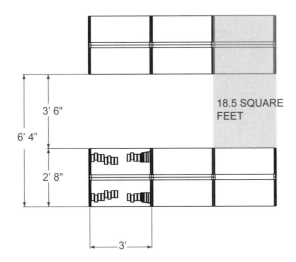

18.5 SQUARE FEET

3' 6"

6' 4"

2' 8"

3'

Albany Molecular Research Library
Used by the permission of Brodart Co.

15" base shelves are mainly utilized for magazines and display shelving.

If utilizing end panels, provide for 2 additional inches at the end of each range.

Provide wider access aisle if top of low adjacent shelf unit is being utilized as a reference counter.

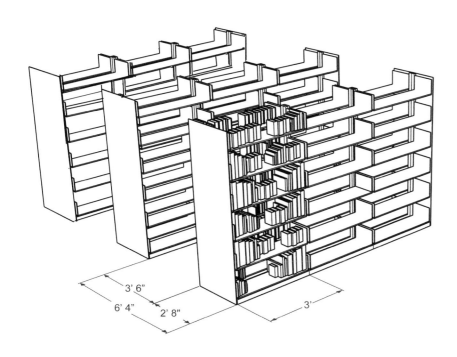

3' 6"

6' 4"

2' 8"

3'

Shelving - 42" Aisle - Base Shelf 15"

18.5 SF

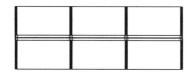

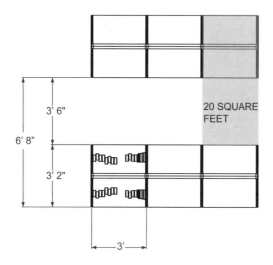

3' 6"

6' 8"

3' 2"

20 SQUARE FEET

3'

Albany Molecular Research Library
Used by the permission of Brodart Co.

18" base shelves are mainly utilized for shelving oversized and folio type materials.

If utilizing end panels, provide for 2 additional inches at the end of each range.

Provide wider access aisle if top of low adjacent shelf unit is being utilized as a reference counter.

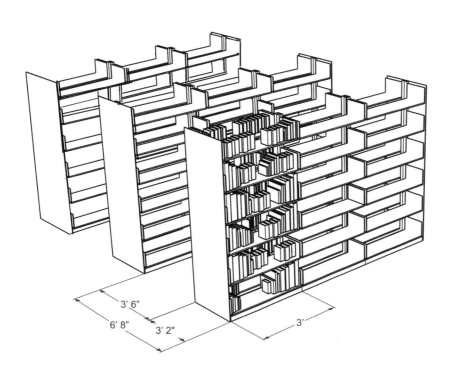

3' 6"

6' 8"   3' 2"   3'

Shelving - 42" Aisle - Base Shelf 18"

20 SF

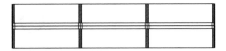

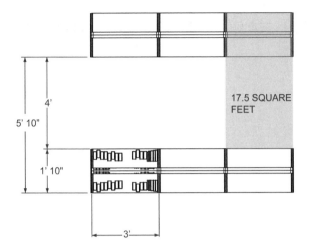

4'

5' 10"

1' 10"

17.5 SQUARE FEET

3'

This is the most prevalent shelving unit for books.

If utilizing end panels, provide for 2 additional inches at the end of each range.

Provide wider access aisle if top of low adjacent shelf unit is being utilized as a reference counter.

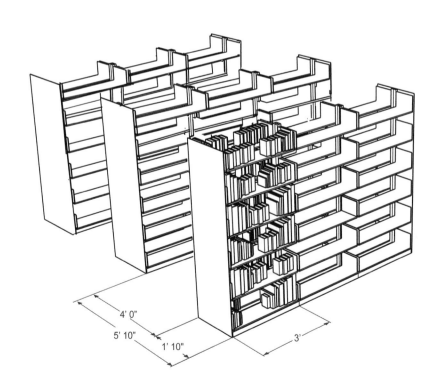

4' 0"

5' 10"

1' 10"

3'

Shelving - 48" Aisle - Base Shelf 10"

17.5 SF

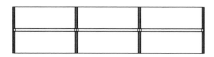

This is the most prevalent unit for picture books.

If utilizing end panels, provide for 2 additional inches at the end of each range.

Provide wider access aisle if top of low adjacent shelf unit is being utilized as a reference counter.

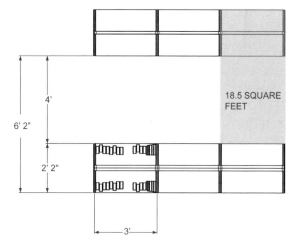

18.5 SQUARE FEET

6' 2"

4'

2' 2"

3'

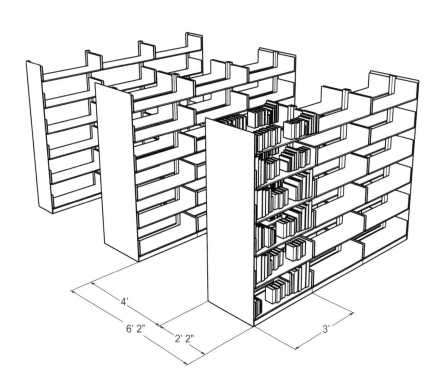

4'

6' 2"

2' 2"

3'

Shelving - 48" Aisle - Base Shelf 12"   18.5 SF

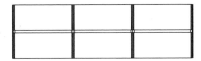

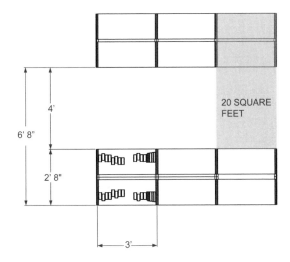

20 SQUARE
FEET

4'

6' 8"

2' 8"

3'

The 15" base shelves are mostly utilized for magazines and display shelving.

If utilizing end panels, provide for 2 additional inches at the end of each range.

Provide wider access aisle if top of low adjacent shelf unit is being utilized as a reference counter.

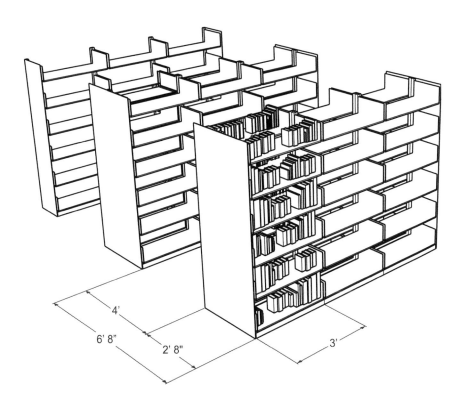

4'

6' 8"

2' 8"

3'

Shelving - 48" Aisle - Base Shelf 15"

20 SF

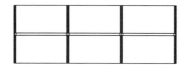

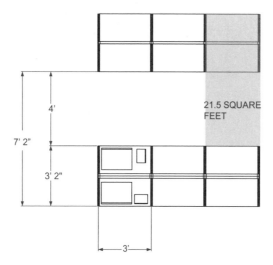

21.5 SQUARE FEET

7' 2"

4'

3' 2"

3'

18" base shelves are mostly utilized for shelving oversized and folio type materials.

If utilizing end panels, provide for 2 additional inches at the end of each range.

Provide wider access aisle if top of low adjacent shelf unit is being utilized as a reference counter.

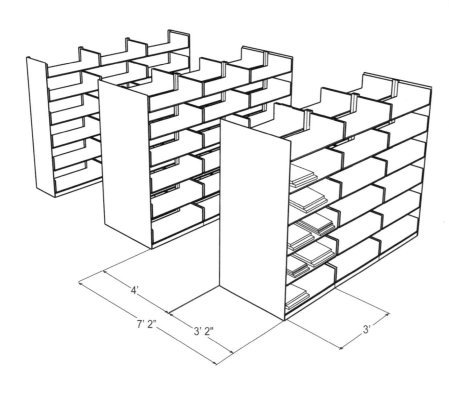

4'

7' 2"

3' 2"

3'

Shelving - 48" Aisle - Base Shelf 18"

21.5 SF

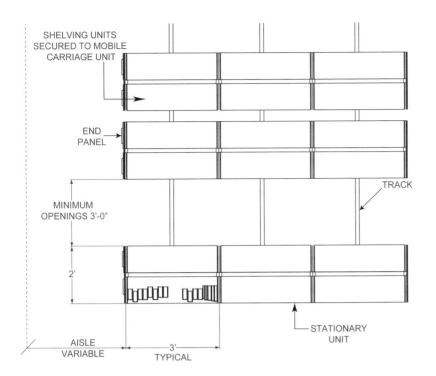

SHELVING UNITS
SECURED TO MOBILE
CARRIAGE UNIT

END
PANEL

TRACK

MINIMUM
OPENINGS 3'-0"

2'

STATIONARY
UNIT

AISLE
VARIABLE

3'
TYPICAL

Elecompack installation at Yale Law School
Used by the permission of Elecompack

In new construction, the optimum track installation is to imbed the track into the floor slab.

Units can operate either manually or electronically.

Track requirements vary by manufacturer.

Each mobile unit rolls along a track system.

Compact storage units are extremely heavy. Consult with a structural engineer to ensure that your floor slab can support the load.

When utilizing end panels, assure that their width is accounted for and provide 36" minimum clearance based upon their sometimes larger depth.

Compact storage units can utilize older, less attractive shelving, as it usually not publicly accessed.

The ratio of static to movable shelving varies. Consult with a shelving manufacturer to define these requirements.

The location of structural columns will dictate the layout of compact storage.

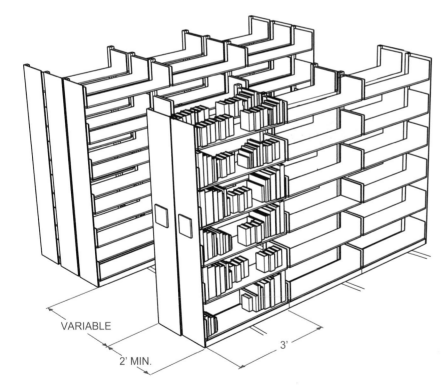

VARIABLE

2' MIN.

3'

Shelving - Compact Double-Faced - Generic

8 SF

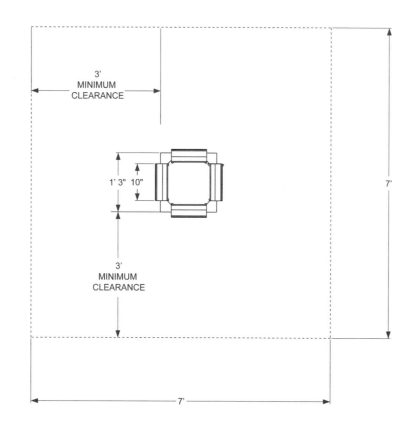

3'
MINIMUM
CLEARANCE

1' 3" 10"

3'
MINIMUM
CLEARANCE

7'

7'

Used by the permission of Brodart Co.

Book display spinners come in a variety of shapes and sizes.

Consider what materials you will display when selecting a unit as they are often media specific.

Provide 36" of clearance around the outside edge of each unit and any adjacent item.

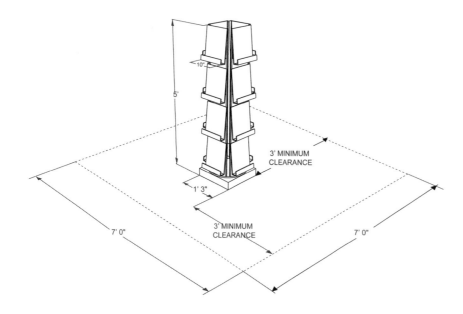

10"

5'

3' MINIMUM
CLEARANCE

1' 3"

3' MINIMUM
CLEARANCE

7' 0"

7' 0"

Spinners

49 SF

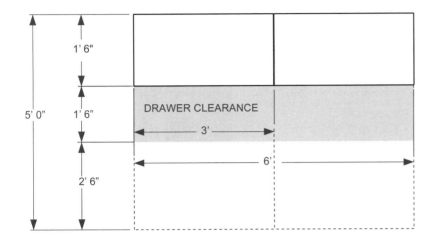

1' 6"

5' 0"

1' 6"

DRAWER CLEARANCE

3'

2' 6"

6'

Used by the permission of Demco, Inc.

Lateral files come in 2, 3, 4 and 5 drawer configurations.

When space is tight, consider placing an overfile storage unit with sliding doors on top of lateral files.

When ganging files together, provide for a minimum of ¼" creep space between each cabinet. In a run of four cabinets, provide 1" additional space.

Lateral files are extremely heavy. Consult with a structural engineer to ensure that your floor slab can support the load.

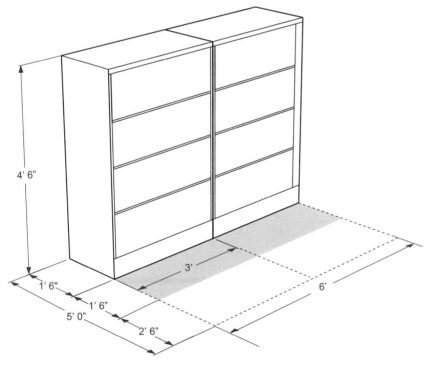

4' 6"

1' 6"

1' 6"

5' 0"

2' 6"

3'

6'

File Cabinets - Lateral

15 SF

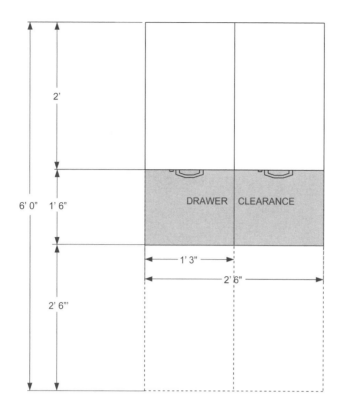

Used by the permission of Demco, Inc.

Vertical files come in 2, 3, 4 and 5 drawer configurations.

When ganging files together, provide for a minimum of ¼" creep space between each cabinet. In a run of four cabinets, provide 1" additional space.

Vertical files are extremely heavy. Consult with a structural engineer to ensure that your floor slab can support the load.

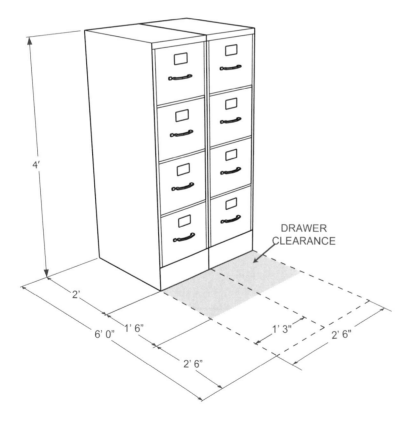

File Cabinets - Vertical

7.5 SF

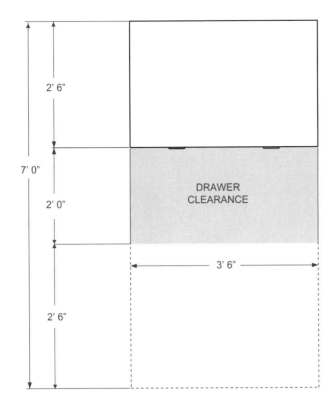

Used by the permission of Demco, Inc.

Provide clearance space in front of map files for drawer to pull out and for a person to stand.

Flat file/map cases are extremely heavy. Consult with a structural engineer to ensure that your floor slab can support the load.

Keep map case top clear to utilize it for reference space.

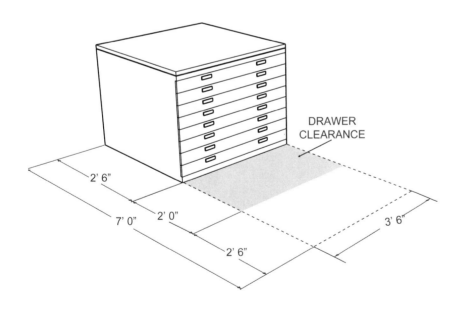

Flat File / Map Case

24SF

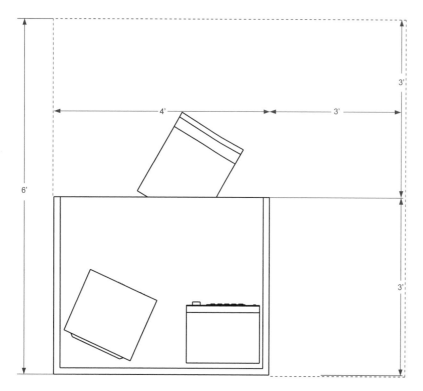

West Chester University
Used by the permission of AGATI Furniture

As a general guideline, single units, as illustrated here, require 3 feet of clearance from table edge to an adjoining aisleway.

Equipment sizes will vary and will change. Determine what equipment will initially be housed at each unit. Provide access to power and data outlets in close proximity to each Audio Station.

Audio stations should be able to accommodate wheelchair bound patrons.

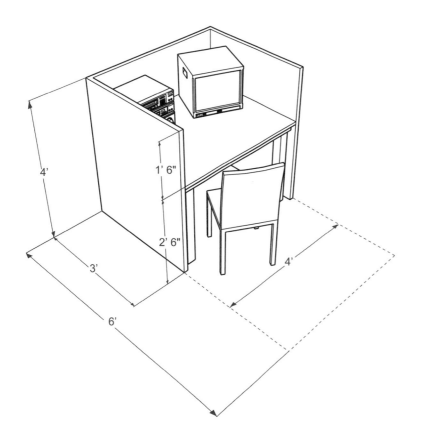

Audio Station - Individual

24 SF

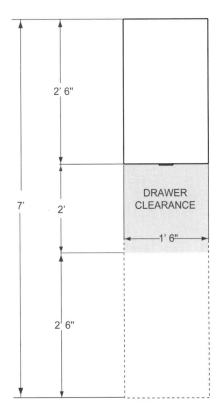

Provide clearance space in front of the microfilm cabinet for drawer to pull out and for a person to stand.

Microform cabinets are extremely heavy. Consult with a structural engineer to ensure that your floor slab can support the load.

If space is limited, consider the use of a high density tape library system. One such system is Gemtrac, which is manufactured by Russ Bassett.

DRAWER CLEARANCE

2' 6"

7'

2'

2' 6"

1' 6"

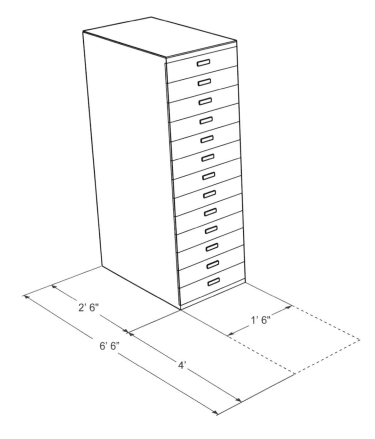

2' 6"

6' 6"

4'

1' 6"

Microform Cabinet - Single Faced   10.5 SF

Reading/Study Areas

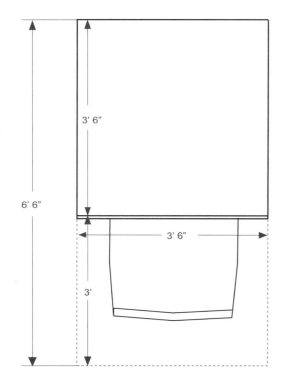

This table type is for individual study.

Table dimensions vary, but 42" x 42" is the recommended size.

Provide 5' clearance from edge of adjacent edge of table.

Provide electrical outlets and data plugs adjacent to or in table.

Tables placed against a wall require less square footage as circulation is only needed on one side.

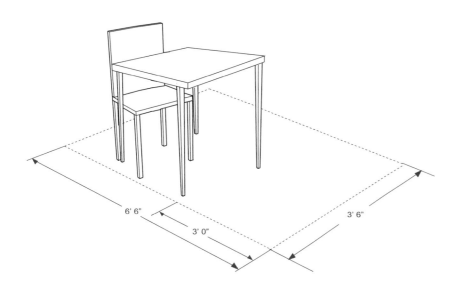

Reading Table - Individual

23 SF

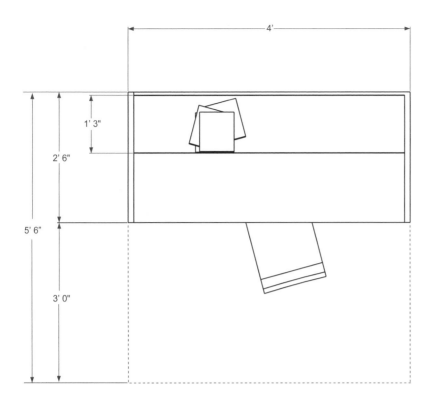

University of Florida, Smathers Library
Gainesville Florida
Used by the permission of AGATI Furniture

To accommodate laptop users provide a minimum of 48" in length.

Provide access to power, data and light.

When placing carrels back to back, provide 5' clearance from table edge to table edge.

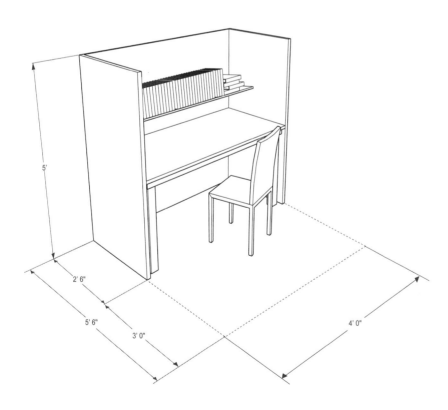

Study Carrel

22 SF

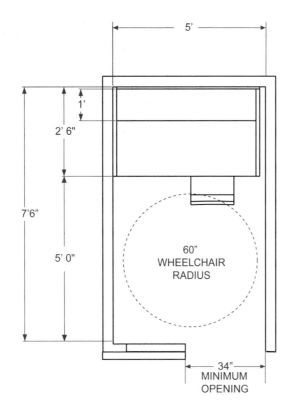

5'

1'

2' 6"

7'6"

5' 0"

60"
WHEELCHAIR
RADIUS

34"
MINIMUM
OPENING

University of Otago Information Services Building
Used by the permission of John Gollings

At a minimum, an enclosed carrel should measure 5' x 7', if it is provided with a sliding door. The work surface in this situation would measure 24" deep.

Any enclosed space must meet ADA guidelines for accessibility.

Enclosed carrels may be fully enclosed with built in walls, or enclosed with systems panels.

Provide electrical outlets and data plugs for portable computers and AV equipment.

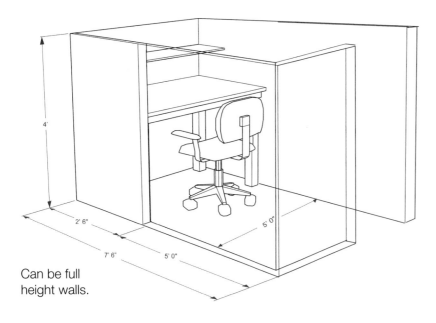

4'

2' 6"

7' 6"

5' 0"

5' 0"

Can be full
height walls.

Carrel - Enclosed

37.5 SF

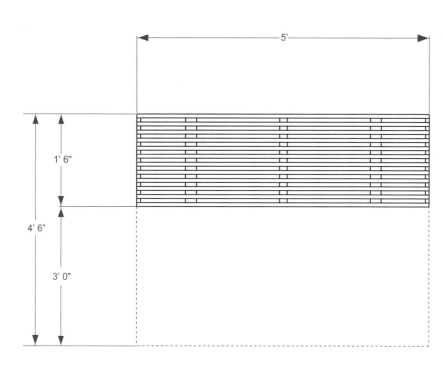

Coralville Public Library
Used by the permission of AGATI Furniture

Place bench along circulation paths or at entry vestibules.

Consider providing cushions for benches.

5'

1' 6"

4' 6"

3' 0"

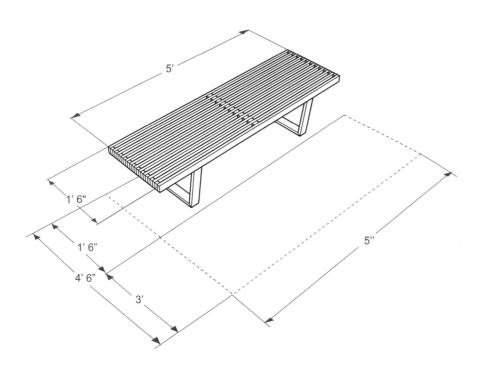

5'

1' 6"

1' 6"

4' 6"

3'

5"

Bench

23 SF

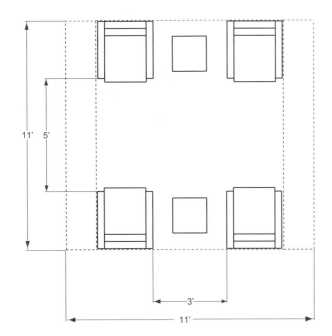

Large chairs are usually placed in groups and may include end tables and coffee tables.

If providing coffee tables add additional square footage.

For individually placed lounge chairs, provide 20 square feet per chair and calculate the table separately.

When placed individually, provide a minimum of 3' circulation space in front of each chair.

The size of lounge chairs can vary greatly. Consult tear sheets of individual chairs being considered for a project to vary square footage requirements.

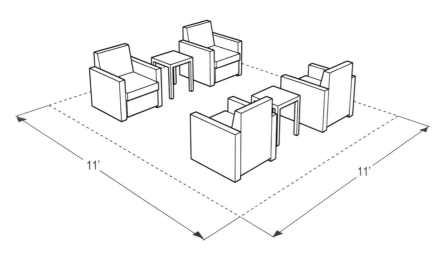

Lounge Chair Grouping

121 SF

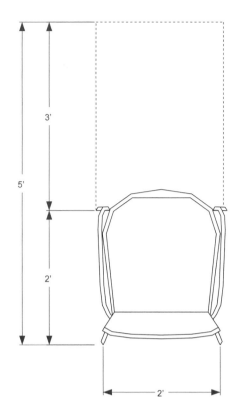

Used by the permission of Demco, Inc.

Provide access aisle through chairs to meet ADA guidelines.

As a general rule of thumb, provide 10 SF per person when calculating the capacity for a meeting room utilizing individual chairs.

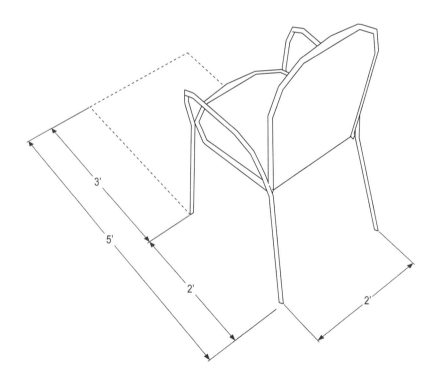

Meeting Room Chair - Stackable   10 SF

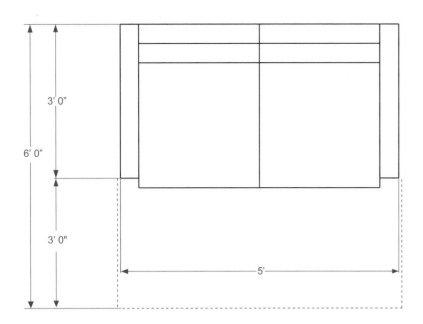

3' 0"

6' 0"

3' 0"

5'

Used by the permission of AGATI Furniture

Sofas are usually placed in groups incorporate end tables, coffee tables, and ottomans. Include additional square footage for these items.

When placed individually provide a minimum of 3' of circulation space in front of each sofa.

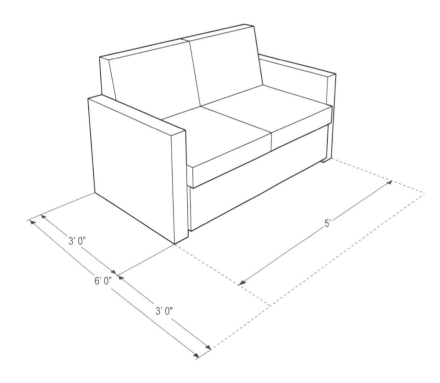

3' 0"

6' 0"

3' 0"

5'

Sofa - Two Person

30 SF

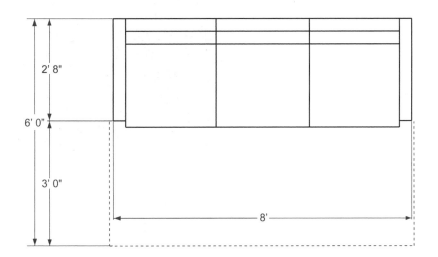

Mira Costa College Information Center
Used by the permission of AGATI Furniture

Sofas are usually placed in groups incorporate end tables, coffee tables, and ottomans. Include additional square footage for these items.

When placed individually provide a minimum of 3' circulation space in front of each sofa.

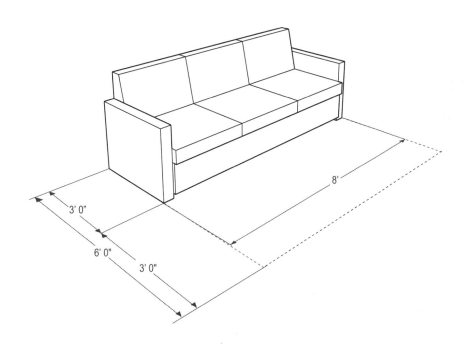

Sofa - Three Person

48 SF

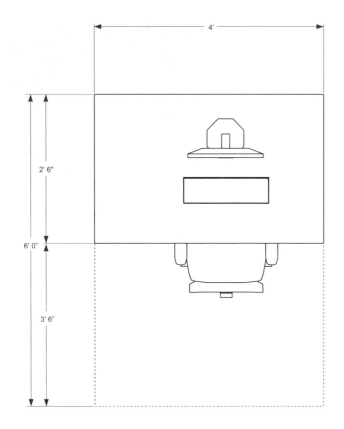

Used by the permission of Demco, Inc.

A 42" wide workstation is acceptable for research, but 48" is preferable.

The width allowed for workstation use may be 36" or even less for stand-up terminals used for quick lookup, such as for a library catalog or end panel PAC.

When PAC's are placed back to back -in this case, across from each other- provide 5' minimum from table edge to table edge.

Patron Access Computer

24 SF

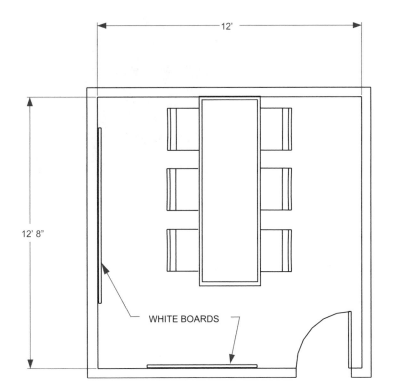

12'

12' 8"

WHITE BOARDS

University of Otago Information Services Building
Used by the permission of John Gollings

As a general rule, provide 25 SF per person to be seated within a group study room.

Provide walls to the ceiling if acoustical separation is desired.

Glass walls to the public area can provide visual control.

Provide electrical outlets and data plugs for portable computer and AV equipment.

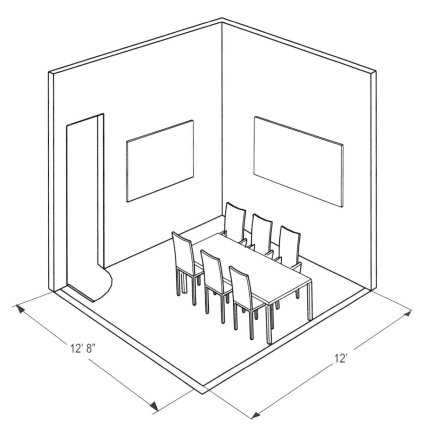

12' 8"

12'

Group Study Room

152 SF

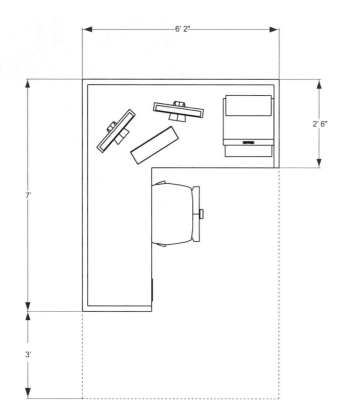

Used by the permission of H3 Hardy Collaboration Architecture

A graphics workstation often has a larger-than-typical monitor, and may include a scanner.

Users may need access to the CPU's CD/DVD drives and USB/Firewire ports.

Provide space for large screen monitors and potentially multiple screens.

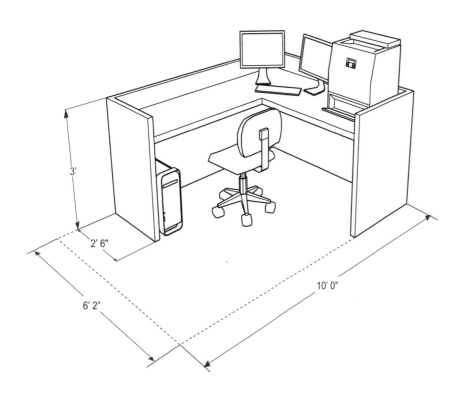

Graphics Workstation

62 SF

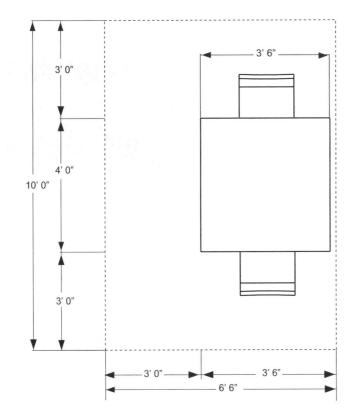

Metropolitan State University
Used by the permission of AGATI Furniture

Provide 5 feet clearance from table edge to table edge when placing tables back to back.

Tables can be placed side to side with minimal clearance when using like-sized tables.

Tables with the legs inset under the table provide more flexibility for groups.

Tables that are 48" wide and have legs at the corners encourage quiet study.

Tables placed against a wall (as shown in the photo above) require less square footage as circulation is needed only on one side.

Provide electrical outlets and data plugs for portable computers and AV equipment.

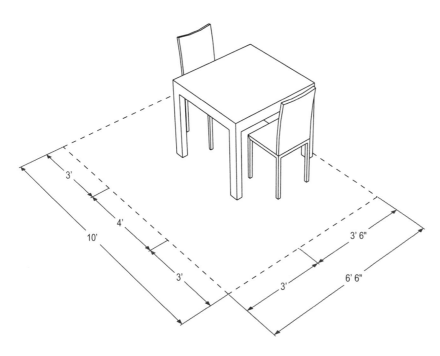

Reading Table - Two-seat (Adult)   66 SF

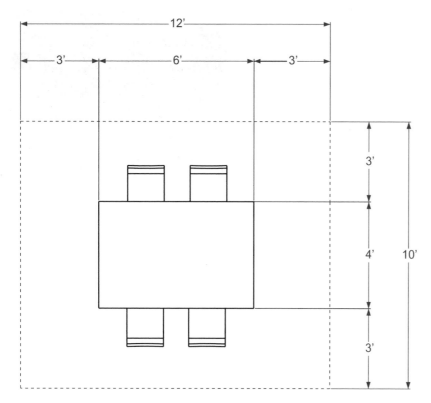

Penn College of Technology
Used by the permission of Brodart Co.

Provide 5 feet clearance from table edge to table edge when placing tables back to back.

Tables can be placed side to side with minimal clearance when using like-sized tables.

Tables with the legs inset under the table provide more flexibility for groups.

Tables that are 48" wide and have legs at the corners encourage quiet study.

Provide electrical outlets and data plugs for portable computers and AV equipment.

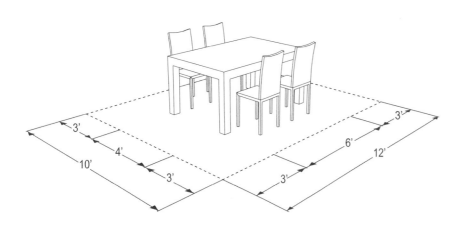

Reading Table - Four-Seat (Adult)

120 SF

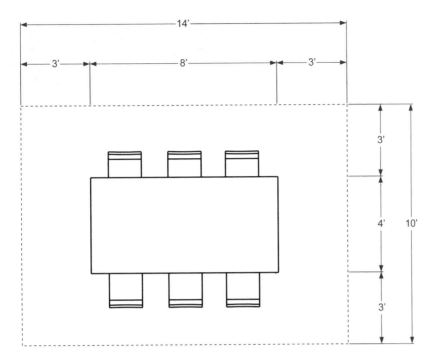

Northlake Community College
Used by the permission of PSA Dewberry

Provide 5 feet clearance from table edge to table edge when placing tables back to back.

Tables can be placed side to side with minimal clearance when using like-sized tables.

Tables with the legs inset under the table (as in the photo above) provide more flexibility for groups.

Tables that are 48" wide and have legs at the corners encourage quiet study.

Provide electrical outlets and data plugs for portable computers and AV equipment.

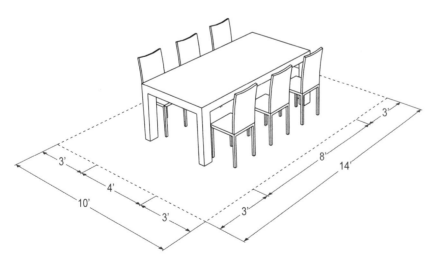

Reading Table - Six-Seat (Adult)

140 SF

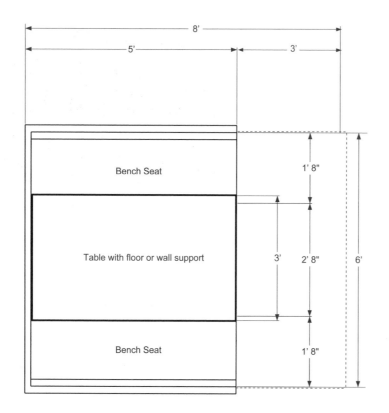

Bench Seat

Table with floor or wall support

Bench Seat

8'

5'

3'

1' 8"

3'

2' 8"

6'

1' 8"

Used by the permission of Demco, Inc.

Tables can be supported by a center post or be wall hung. Booth seating encourages casual collaboration. There are many different shapes and sizes for booths.

Provide electrical outlets and data plugs for portable computers and AV equipment.

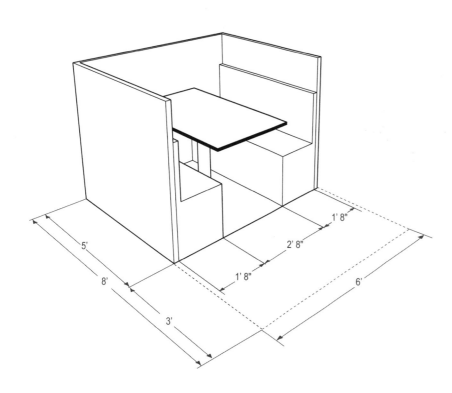

1' 8"

2' 8"

1' 8"

6'

5'

8'

3'

Reading Table - Booth Seating

48 SF

Equipment

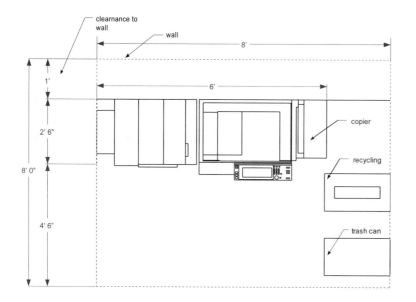

clearnance to wall

wall

8'

1'

6'

2' 6"

8' 0"

4' 6"

copier

recycling

trash can

Used by the permission of H3 Hardy Collaboration Architecture

Provide adequate space to provide access to paper trays and for maintenance of the machines.

Provide a nearby space for paper collating

Allow for an adjacent space for a vending station if one is used with the copier system.

Check with your vendor to see if a clearance space is needed behind the copier to dissipate heat.

Provide enough space for large recycle bins and trash cans near every copier.

Shelving or book trucks are needed adjacent to copiers for return materials.

Data and power on dedicated circuits.

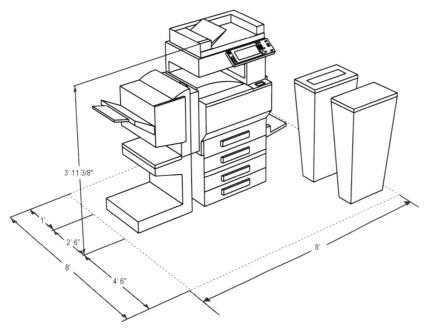

3' 11 3/8"

1'

2' 6"

8'

4' 6"

8'

Stand-Alone Copier/Printer/Scanner

64 SF

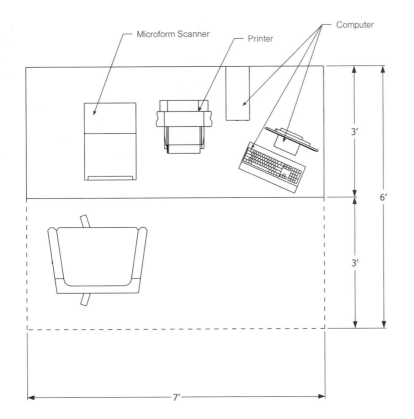

Microform Scanner Printer Computer

3'
6'
3'
7'

Microform equipment is often very heavy. Utilize a table that is sturdy enough to hold it.

Often the vendor of the machine will sell a suitable table that is designed to be used with the machine.

When placing microform equipment, provide adequate service space on all sides.

Locate microform equipment close to a change machine or value added machine.

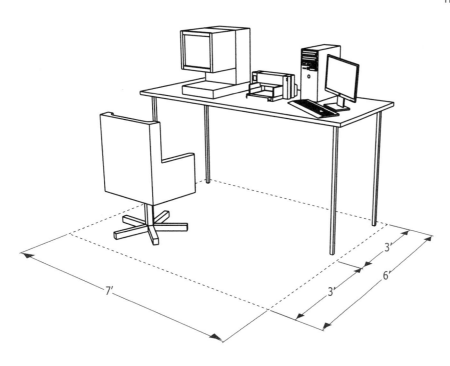

7'
3'
3'
6'

Microform Scanner/Printer (with Computer)

42 SF

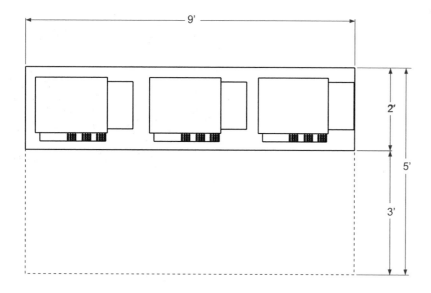

The printer area can be either a table or a counter.

The printer may be stand alone unit or a counter top model.

Allow room for a release station. This may be a small unit attached to the printer, or a CPU and screen.

Provide power and data to allow networking.

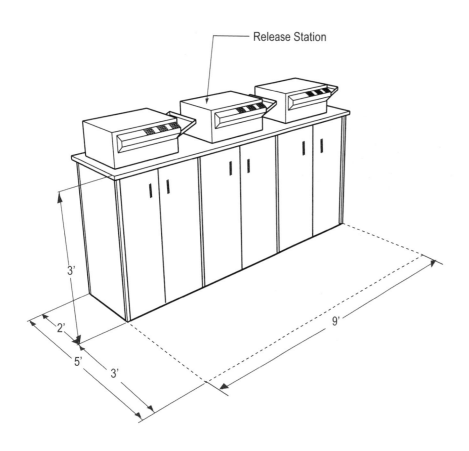

Release Station

Print Station

45 SF

Children's Areas - Specialized Functions

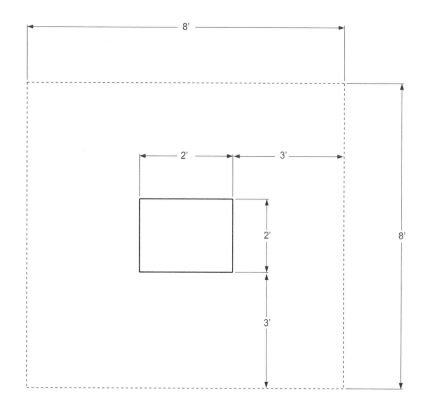

Used by the permission of Demco, Inc.

Open space allows you to have an activity area.

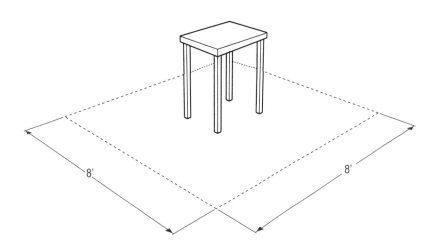

Activity Table Area

64 SF

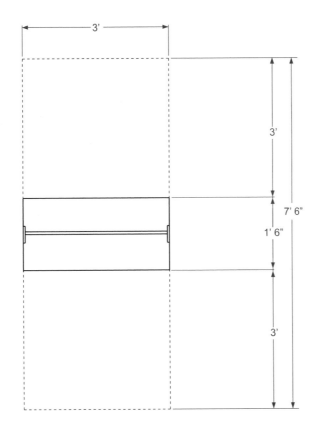

Used by the permission of Demco, Inc.

Book kits are often incorporated into the shelving ranges.

The same unit can be single sided or double sided.

Coordinate the diameter of the unit's horizontal rod with the diameter of the hanging bag hooks.

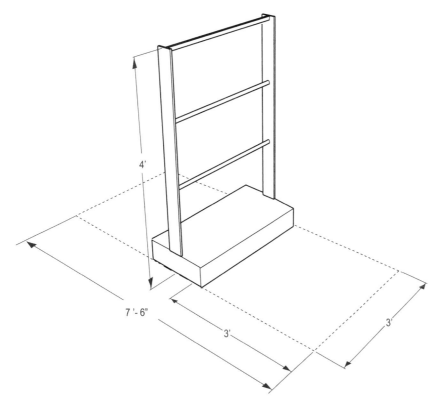

Media Hanging Kits

23 SF

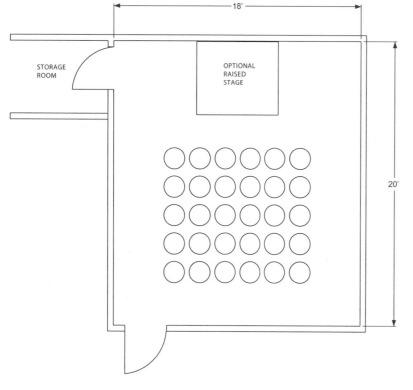

STORAGE ROOM

OPTIONAL RAISED STAGE

18'

20'

Live Oak Library, Savannah, Georgia
Used by the permission of Malcolm Holzman

This sketch shows a program room for 30 children.

Program rooms should connect to a storage area for props and supplies.

Consider planning a counter with sink adjacent to this space.

As a general requirement, provide 12 square feet of space for each of the room's occupants.

If planning for a puppet stage, provide additional square footage for stage and storage.

Provide for stroller parking adjacent to the program room.

Provide for a coat rack adjacent to the program room.

Consider having view windows into the program room for waiting parents.

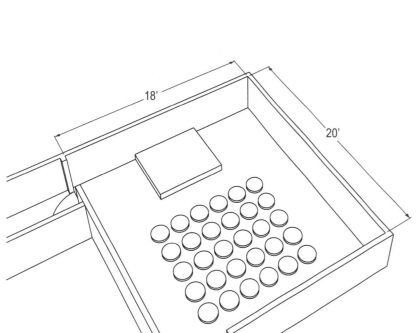

18'

20'

Children's Storytelling / Program Room

360 SF

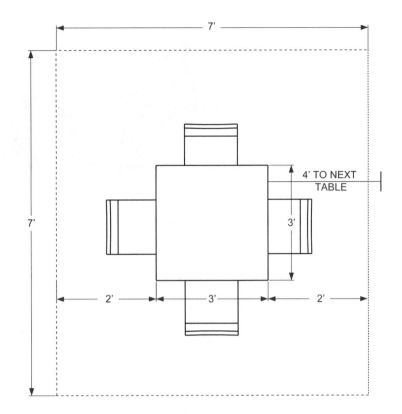

4' TO NEXT TABLE

7'

7'

3'

2'

3'

2'

Used by the permission of Brodart Co.

Children's tables and chairs come in a variety of table and seat heights.

Table heights vary from 21" high for toddler size to approximately 28" for middle school size.

Coordinate the chair and table heights.

When laying out multiples tables, provide four feet minimum clearance from table edge to table edge.

	TABLE	SEAT HIGHT
CHILD SIZE	20"	12"
JUVENILE SIZE	25"	14"
YOUTH SIZE	27"	16"

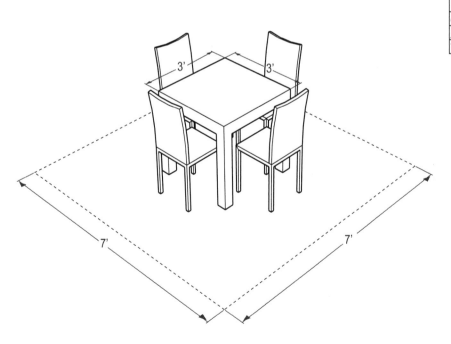

3'

3'

7'

7'

Four Seat Table - Child Sized

49 SF

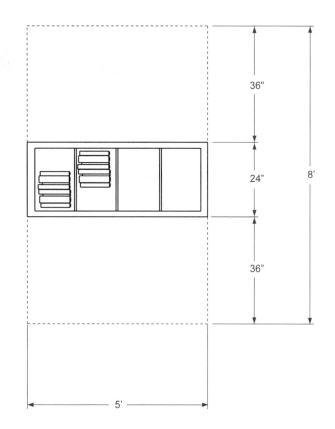

Tuckahoe Area Library, Richmond Virginia
Used by the permission of PSA-Dewberry

Match the height of the bins or racks to the approximate height of the children who will be using the books.

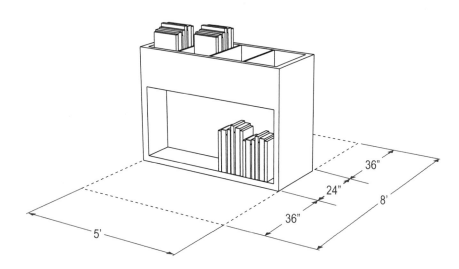

Picture Book Bins / Rack

40 SF

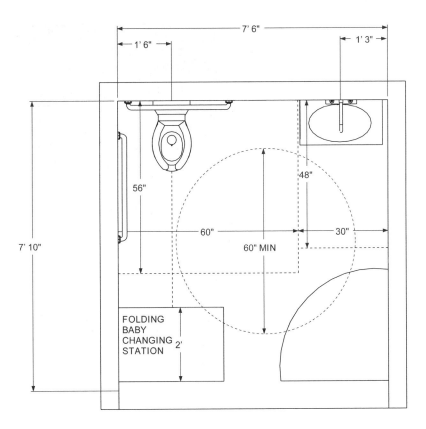

Keller Public Library
Used by the permission of PSA-Dewberry

Family restrooms should provide a fold-down baby changing station or stationary counter.

Consider providing a wall mounted safety seat for securing toddlers.

Provide a large sized garbage can with lid within this toilet.

Family restrooms should provide a folding baby changing station or stationary counter.

Consider providing a wall mounted safety seat for securing toddlers.

Provide a large sized garbage can with lid within this toilet area.

Restrooms are usually included in the net to gross area. Family restrooms are often in excess of the code required toilets.

Public libraries may consider adding space for a chair or bench to provide a space for nursing mothers.

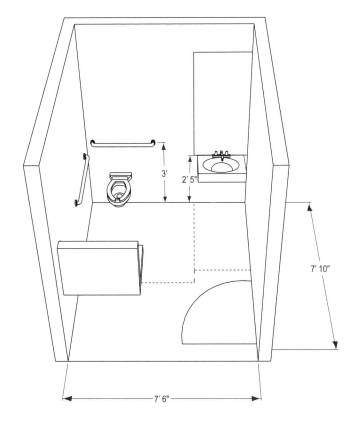

Restroom - Family (ADA Accessible)   59 SF

Staff Areas

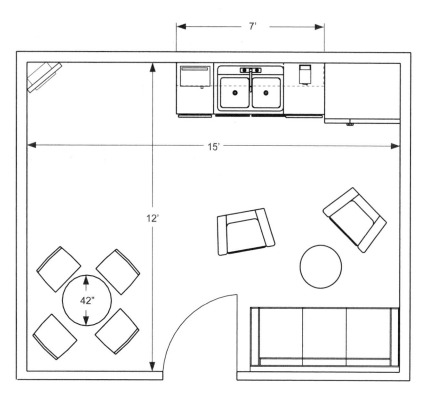

Used by the permission of Hedrich Blessing Photographers

The size of the break room depends upon the size of the library staff.

As a general rule of thumb, provide 25 square feet for each person to be seated in the break room at one time.

Provide wireless connection for staff members to use computers during break.

Larger staff break rooms may often include a vending area.

In larger break rooms, consider adding a counter as a divider between the pantry area and the seating area.

Consult ADA guidelines for required clearance at the sink area.

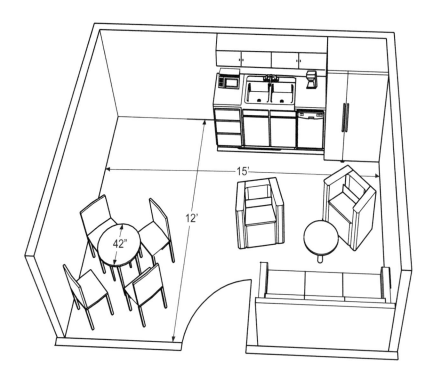

Break Room

180 SF

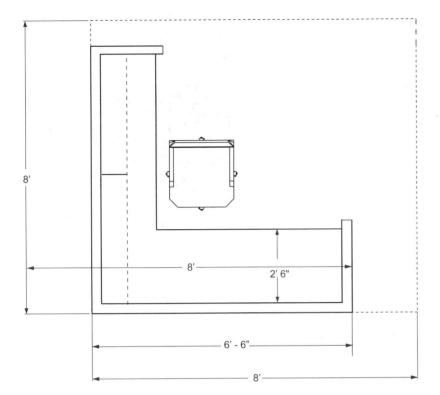

Used by the permission of PSA-Dewberry

Size varies greatly depending on the space available and work done at the workstation.

Allow space around the workstation for book trucks when needed.

The height of the dividing panels varies according to the need for privacy, transparency, and quiet work areas.

Power and data may be run through the workstation, but needs to be provided through floor or wall outlets.

As a minimum, provide a 7' x 7' workstation for each circulation staff member and a 10' x 10' workstation for each technical services staff member.

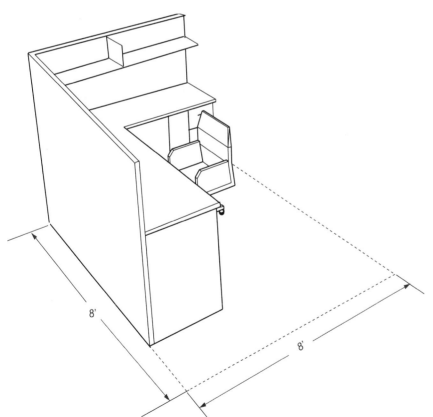

Single Staff Workstation

64 SF

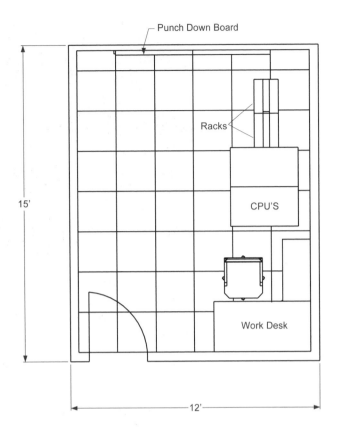

Punch Down Board

Racks

CPU'S

15'

Work Desk

12'

Rockwall County Library, Texas
Used by the permission of PSA-Dewberry

The size of this room can vary greatly and is dependant upon the size of the library.

Server rooms may require a raised floor to facilitate changes to the cabling system.

Server rooms will require a supplemental air conditioning unit to maintain constant temperature and humidity control.

An uninterrupted power source is often needed in a server room to facilitate shutdown of the server during a power outage.

One wall of the server room should be a plywood punch-down board for cable management.

A repair table is often located in the server room.

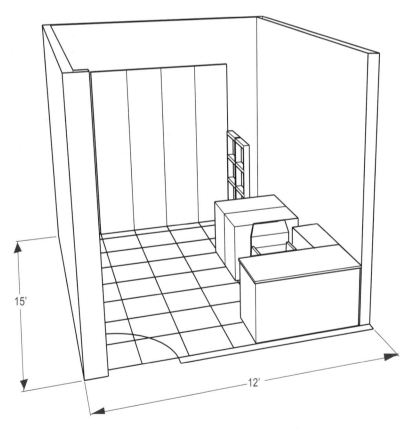

15'

12'

Server Room

180 SF

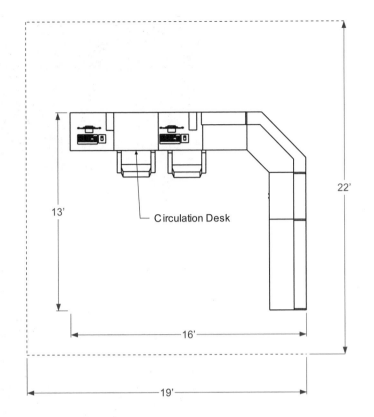

13'

22'

── Circulation Desk

16'

19'

Sun Prairie Public Library

Carefully consider equipment being used at the desk to determine size, design and storage.

Design the desk to be as flexible as possible as equipment and functions will change every few years.

Consider designing desk to accommodate self check out units as well as manned stations.

Design the desk height to work for the majority of the staff.

Provide space for book trucks and shelving behind the desk.

Consider mocking up the desk with all proposed equipment to define your desk square footage needs.

As a rule of thumb typical heights for reference and circulation desks are as follows:
Standing Height Counter- 42" (range 39"-42")
Seating Height Counter- 32" (range 30"-34")
ADA compliant counter height- 34" maximum (verify with your local ADA code requirements)

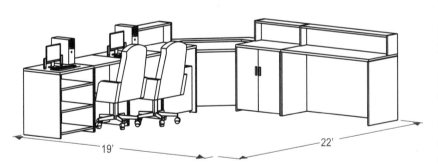

19'

22'

Circulation / Check In - Check Out

418 SF

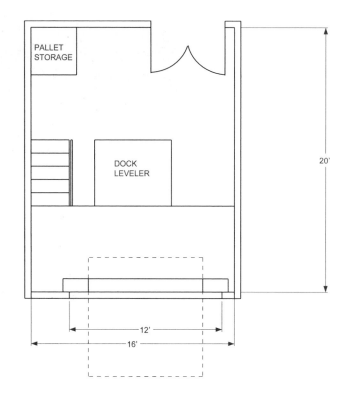

Rockwall County Library, Texas
Used by the permission of Denelle
Wrightston

William T. Young Library at the University
of Kentucky, Lexington, KY
Used by the permission of Mary McLaren

Area depicted is for a single bay
loading dock.

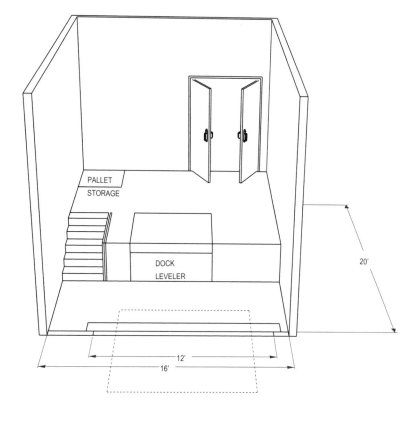

Loading Dock

320 SF

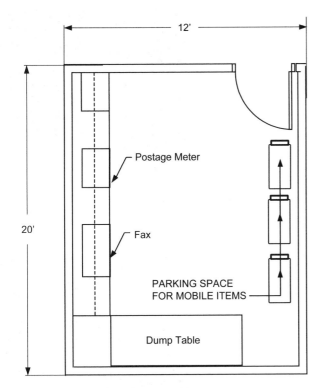

12'

20'

Postage Meter

Fax

PARKING SPACE
FOR MOBILE ITEMS

Dump Table

*William T. Young Library at the University
of Kentucky, Lexington, KY
Used by the permission of Mary McLaren*

The size of the mail room may vary greatly, depending on the size of your library facility.

At a minimum, the mail room should include a dump table or counter top for mail sorting, mail sort bins, a postage meter, a scale and storage for supplies.

If providing Interlibrary Loan, provide a designated space for outgoing and incoming book bins within the mail room

Within the mail room, provide for permanent parking spaces for the mail cart, dollies, hand trucks, book trucks and all other wheeled equipment.

The mail room may also contain a fax machine and a copier. Expand your square footage to include these items.

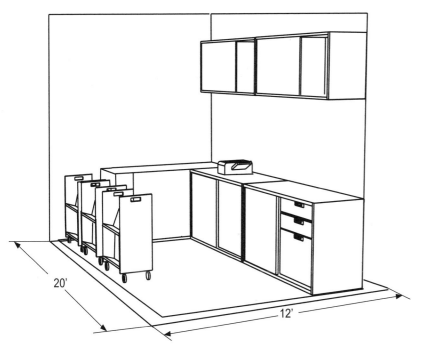

20'

12'

Mail Room

240 SF

Offices

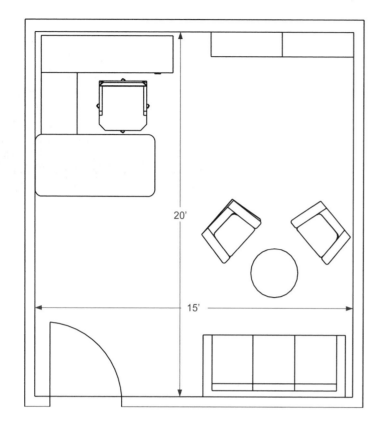

Rockwall Public Library, Texas
Used by the permission of PSA-Dewberry

Work space should include desk with locked file drawers, a work counter, and an ergonomic computer workstation with a dedicated printer/scanner.

Include vertical or lateral file cabinets for a variety of file types.

Provide comfortable seating for conversation e.g. sofa, lounge chairs and coffee table.

Include a 4 to 6 person table for small group meetings.

Provide bookcases and wall mounted display shelving to display awards, etc.

Some director's offices have a dedicated restroom including a shower for the director's use.

Provide space to hang guests' coats, either a coat rack or a closet.

Office should be located adjacent to executive secretary or administrative assistant and in proximity to direct reports.

Consider providing a wall mounted LCD-TV.

Provide power and data outlets throughout the office.

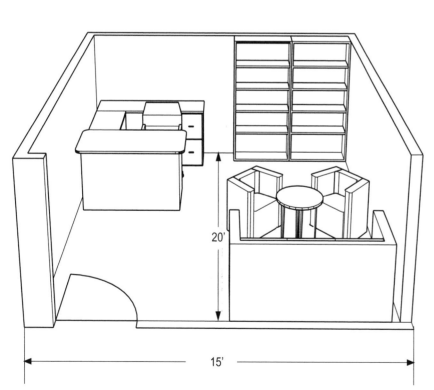

Director's Office

300 SF

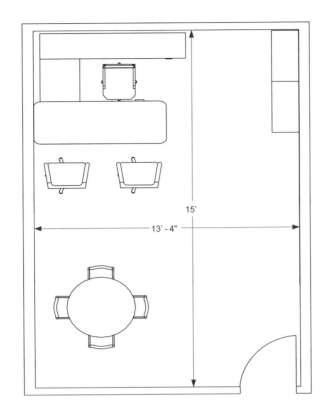

New York School of Interior Design
Used by the permission of H3 Hardy Collaboration
Architecture

Work space should include an ergonomic U-shaped desk with locked file drawers and a computer workstation.

Provide two seats on the other side of the staff desk for visitors or other staff.

Include a 4 person table for small group meetings.

Vertical or lateral file cabinets may be needed.

Provide wall mounted bookshelves.

Provide a coat rack to hang coats.

Consider placement of power and data outlets throughout the room.

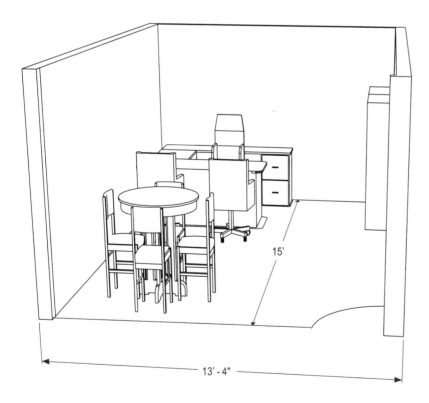

Staff Office - Large

200 SF

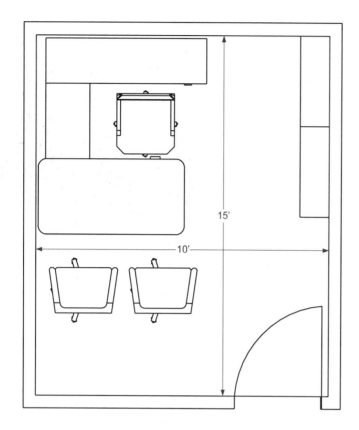

New York Academy of Sciences
Used by the permission of H3 Hardy Collaborationi
Architecture

Work space should include an ergonomic U-shaped desk with locked file drawers and a computer workstation.

Provide two seats on the other side of the staff desk for visitors or other staff.

Include a 4 person table for small group meetings.

Vertical or lateral file cabinets may be needed.

Provide wall mounted bookshelves.

Provide a coat rack to hang coats.

Consider placement of power and data outlets throughout the room.

Offices for Children's Librarians may require additional storage space, e.g. cabinets and shelving.

Offices in the Technical Services area may require room for book trucks.

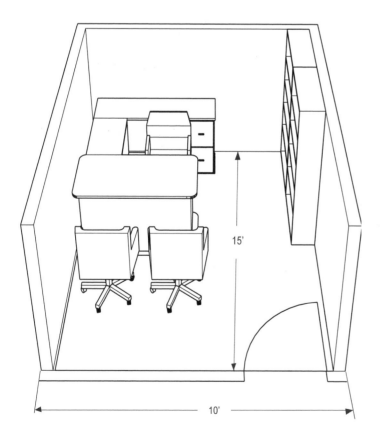

Staff Office - Medium

150 SF

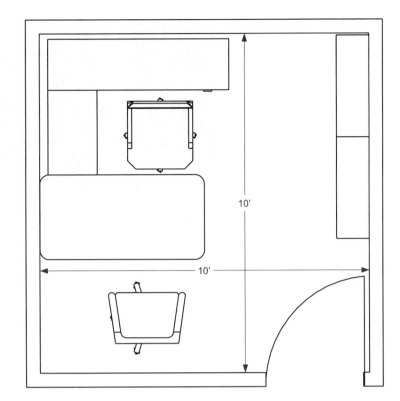

Used by the permission of Brodart Brodart Co.

Work space should include an ergonomic U-shaped desk with locked file drawers and acomputer workstation.

Provide one seat on the other side of the staff desk for visitors or other staff.

Vertical or lateral file cabinets may be needed.

Wall mounted bookshelves may be needed.

Provide a coat rack to hang coats

Provide adequate power and data outlets.

Offices for Children's Librarian may require additional storage space, e.g. cabinets and shelving

Offices in the Technical Services area may require room for book trucks.

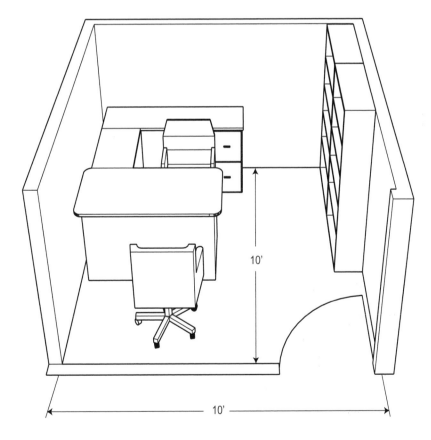

Staff Office - Small

100 SF

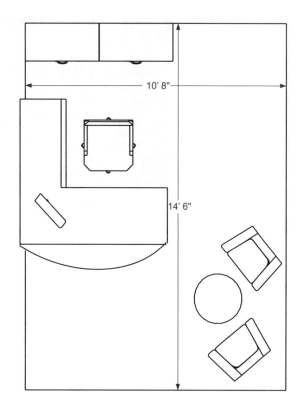

AT&T Reception
Used by the permission of AGATI Furniture

The transaction ledge is a place for patrons to sign in and out. The transaction ledge can also be used for departmental functions - for instance, in and out boxes.

10' 8"

14' 6"

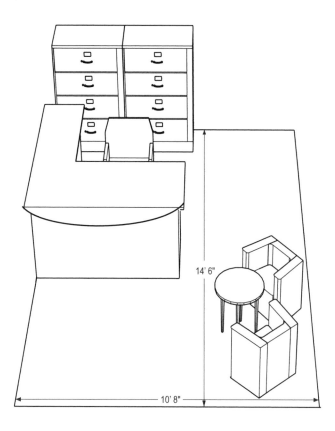

14' 6"

10' 8"

Reception Area

154 SF

SYSTEM PANELS

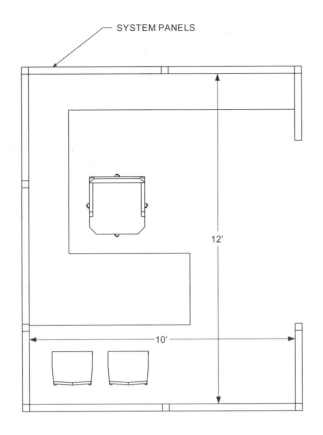

12'

10'

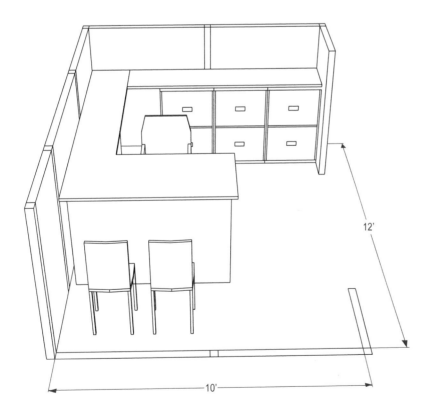

12'

10'

Used by the permission of Brodart Brodart Co.

Size varies greatly depending on the space available and work done at the station.

Allow space around the workstation for book trucks as needed.

The height of the dividing panels varies according to the need for privacy, transparency, and quiet work areas.

System panels can support the distribution of power and data wiring to outlets at the workstation. However, the feed into the systems panel will occur through a wall outlet or floor box.

Supervisor Workstation

120 SF

Working / Sorting

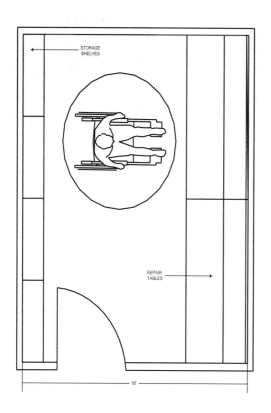

*William T. Young Library at the University
of Kentucky, Lexington, KY
Used by the permission of Mary McLaren*

The equipment repair room should be located adjacent to the IT department, as it is primarily used for computer repair.

Provide plenty of outlets and internet connections. Consider providing these at work counter height.

Provide a variety of depths and heights of shelving.

Consider the notes about the server room if the equipment repair room is going to be used to fix computers.

The equipment room is usually a part of the IT Department.

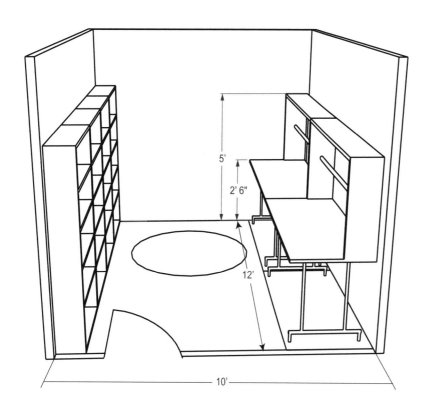

Equipment Repair Room

120 SF

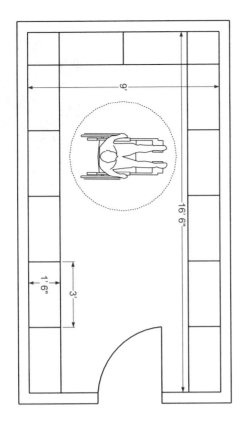

William T. Young Library at the University
of Kentucky, Lexington, KY
Used by the permission of Mary McLaren

Provide a variety of depths of shelving units for housing different supplies.

Provide open floor space for storage of boxes and palettes of materials.

All enclosed rooms must meet ADA requirements.

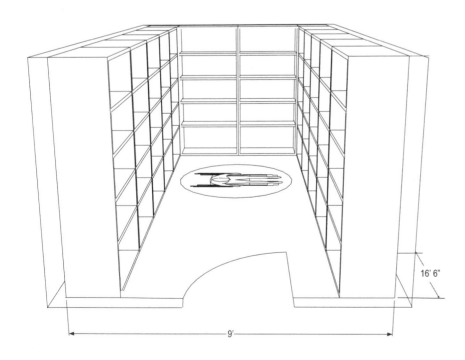

Supply Room   150 SF

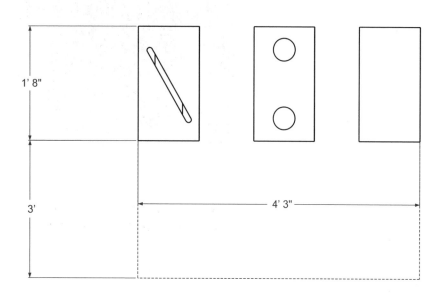

1' 8"

3'

4' 3"

Used by the permission of Brodart Co.

Provide multiple bins for glass, paper, aluminum and plastic.

If you allow food and drink in your library, you may need more units.

Provide recycling containers near all vending areas.

Provide recycling containers in multiple locations, especially at the entrance to your building.

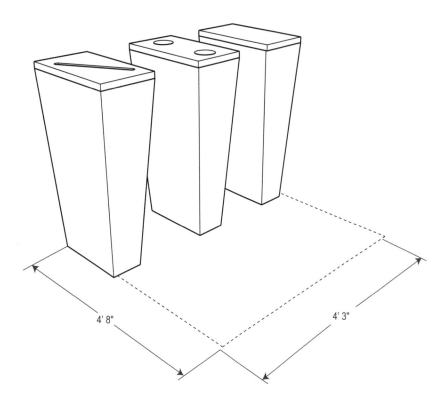

4' 8"

4' 3"

Recycling Containers

20 SF

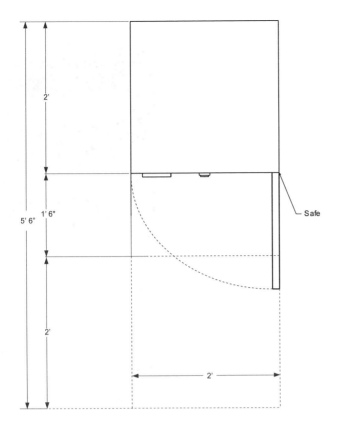

Used by the permission of H3 Hardy Collaboration Architecture

Safes can be wall mounted, floor mounted or table mounted. Consider your needs when planning for a safe.

For smaller needs, consider providing a wall mounted safe for ease of access.

If your safe is an electronic model, provide an adjacent power outlet.

Safes can be extremely heavy. Consult your structural engineer to assess the floor loading capability.

Provide adequate light source to view contents of the safe.

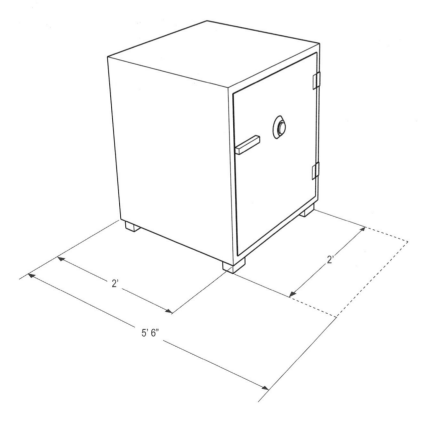

Safe   11 SF

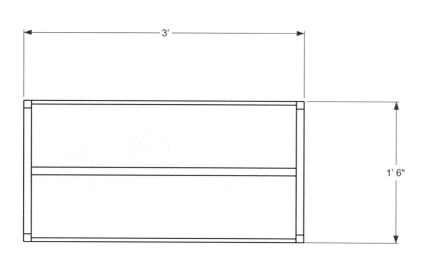

Used by the permission of Demco, Inc.

All mobile units require permanent parking spaces.

Check with your library for their standard size book truck.

Consider where you will park your book trucks when not in use, as this will add square footage to that particular department.

Allow space for book trucks at the circulation desk.

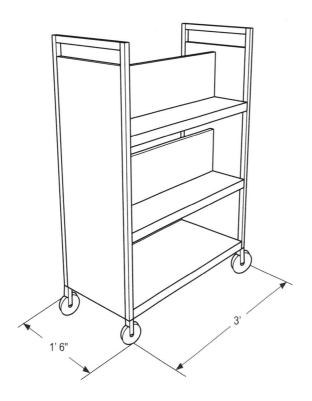

Book Truck

4.5 SF

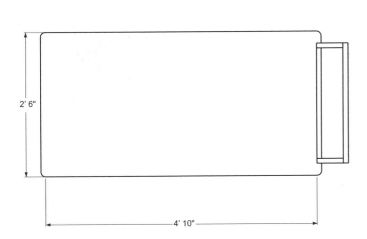

All mobile units require permanent parking spaces.

Flat Truck

12 SF

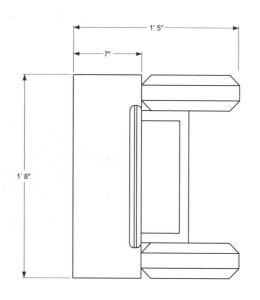

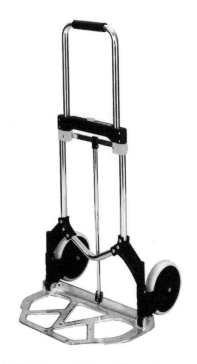

Used by the permission of Demco, Inc.

All mobile units require permanent parking spaces.

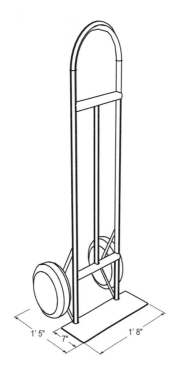

Hand Truck / Dolly

3 SF

Used by the permission of Brodart Co.

All mobile units require permanent parking spaces.

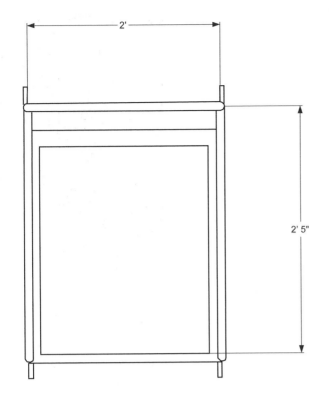

2'

2' 5"

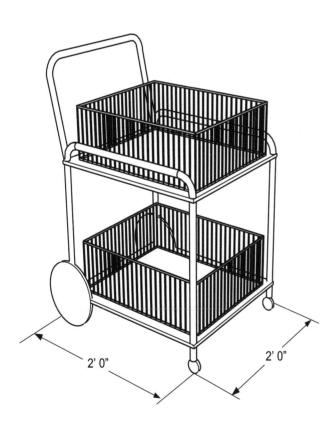

2' 0"

2' 0"

Mail Delivery Cart

5 SF

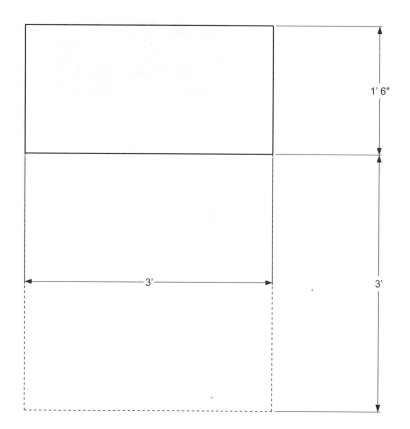

1' 6"

3'

3'

Used by the permission of Demco, Inc.

Depths vary dependent on what you are storing.

Aisle widths need to be wider if shelves are deeper.

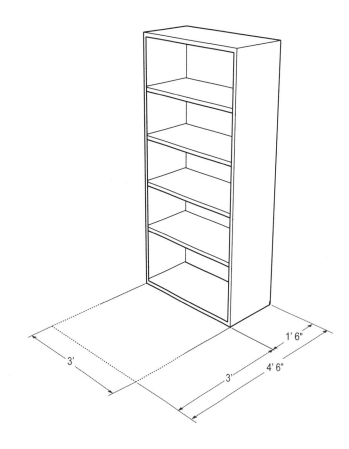

1' 6"

3'

3'

4' 6"

Supply / Storage Closet Cabinet or Shelf Unit

14 SF

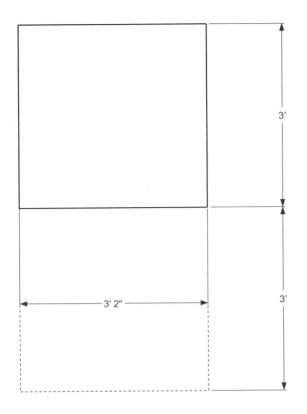

3'

3' 2"

3'

William T. Young Library at the University of Kentucky, Lexington, KY
Used by the permission of Mary McLaren

Vending machines are usually provided by the snack vendor. Check with vendor for specifics of sizes.

Many libraries are adding coffee service machines which require water and power sources.

Academic libraries often require data input for card swipes.

Vending machines can be color coordinated to match your interior design.

Provide air space at the back of each vending machine.

Check with vendors for footprint of each machine.

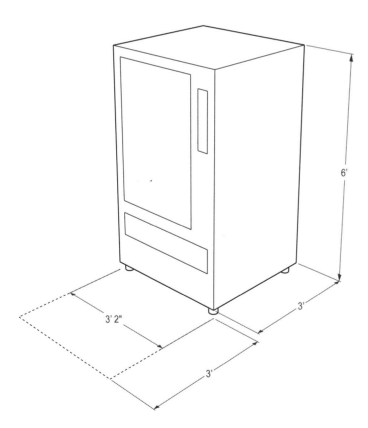

6'

3'

3' 2"

3'

Vending Machine

19 SF

Room Name

IDENTIFICATION	
Department Name	
Room #	
SIZE	
Proposed NSF	
Special Dimensons	
USE	
Primary Activities	
Frequency/Hours	
Access	
RELATIONSHIPS	
Adjacencies	
Proximities	
Floor Level Location	
CHARACTERISTICS	
Ceiling Height	
Ceiling Finish	
Floor Finish	
Wall Finish	
Acoustical Treatments	
Special Requirements	
MECHANICAL AND	
ELECTRICAL	
Natural Lighting	
Artificial Lighting	
HVAC	
Plumbing	
Electrical Power	
Security	
Communication	
EQUIPMENT AND	
FURNISHINGS	
Project Name	
Project Location	

Program Data Sheet

Date: _____

FURNITURE & EQUIPMENT SCHEDULE

Room Name _____

Room # _____

EQUIPMENT DESCRIPTION	ASF	TOTAL	QUANTITY	NEW	EXIST'G	FIXED	MOVABLE	LENGTH	WIDTH	HEIGHT
				O	O	O	O			
				O	O	O	O			
				O	O	O	O			
				O	O	O	O			
				O	O	O	O			
				O	O	O	O			
				O	O	O	O			
				O	O	O	O			
				O	O	O	O			
				O	O	O	O			
				O	O	O	O			
				O	O	O	O			
				O	O	O	O			
				O	O	O	O			
				O	O	O	O			
				O	O	O	O			
				O	O	O	O			
				O	O	O	O			
				O	O	O	O			
				O	O	O	O			
				O	O	O	O			
				O	O	O	O			
				O	O	O	O			
				O	O	O	O			
				O	O	O	O			
				O	O	O	O			
				O	O	O	O			
				O	O	O	O			
				O	O	O	O			
				O	O	O	O			
				O	O	O	O			
				O	O	O	O			
				O	O	O	O			
				O	O	O	O			
				O	O	O	O			
				O	O	O	O			
				O	O	O	O			
				O	O	O	O			
				O	O	O	O			
				O	O	O	O			
				O	O	O	O			
				O	O	O	O			
				O	O	O	O			
				O	O	O	O			
				O	O	O	O			
				O	O	O	O			
				O	O	O	O			
				O	O	O	O			
				O	O	O	O			
				O	O	O	O			

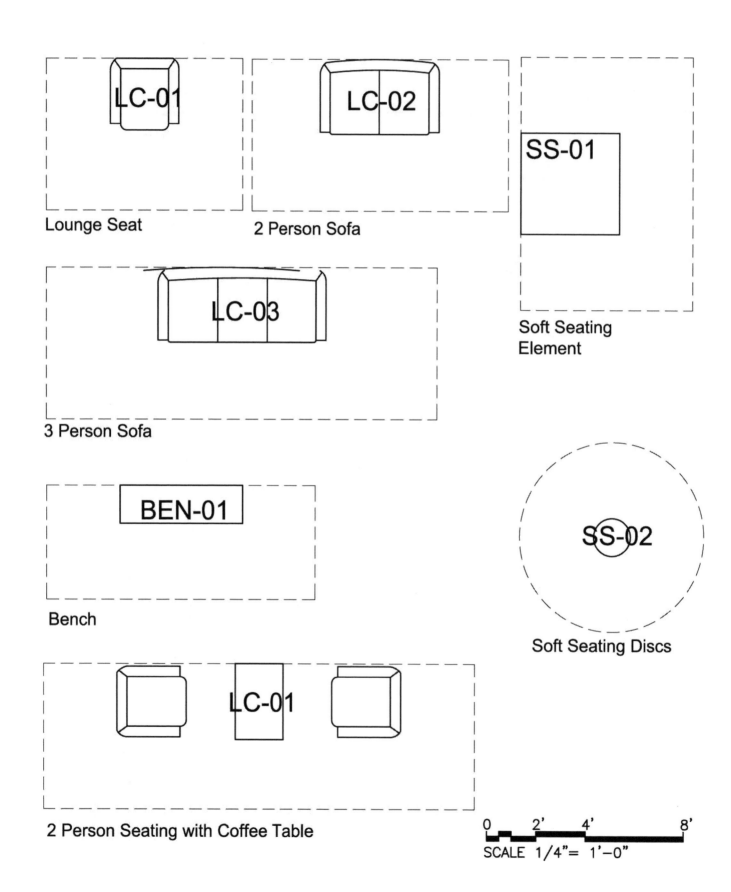

LC-01

Lounge Seat

LC-02

2 Person Sofa

SS-01

Soft Seating
Element

LC-03

3 Person Sofa

BEN-01

Bench

SS-02

Soft Seating Discs

LC-01

2 Person Seating with Coffee Table

0   2'   4'   8'
SCALE 1/4"= 1'-0"

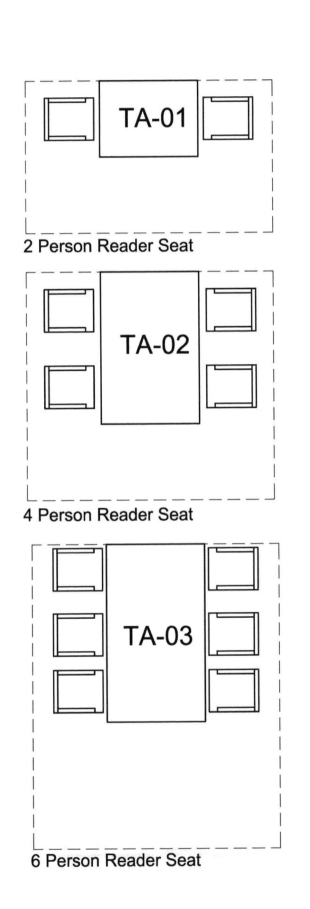

TA-01

2 Person Reader Seat

TA-02

4 Person Reader Seat

TA-03

6 Person Reader Seat

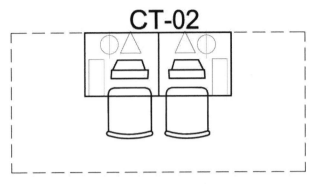

CT-02

2 Person Computer Table

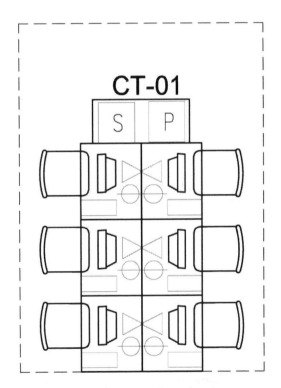

CT-01

6 Person Computer Table

0   2'   4'   8'

SCALE 1/4"= 1'-0"

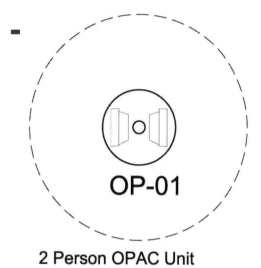

OP-01

2 Person OPAC Unit

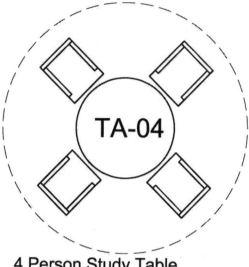

TA-04

4 Person Study Table

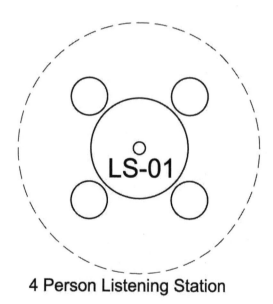

LS-01

4 Person Listening Station

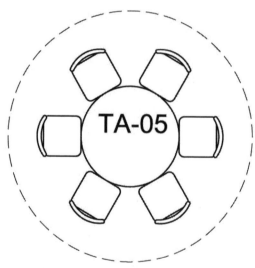

TA-05

6 Person Banquet Table

```
0        2'      4'              8'
```

SCALE 1/4"= 1'-0"

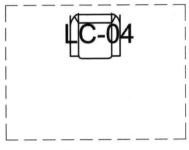

LC-04

Children's Lounge Seat

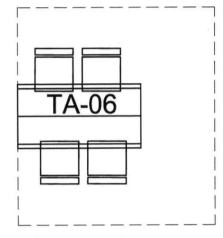

TA-06

4 Person Children's
Reader Table

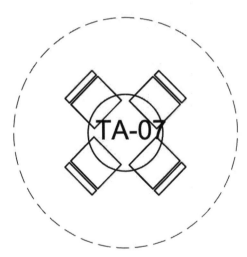

TA-07

4 Person Children's
Reader Table

0   2'   4'   8'

SCALE 1/4"= 1'-0"

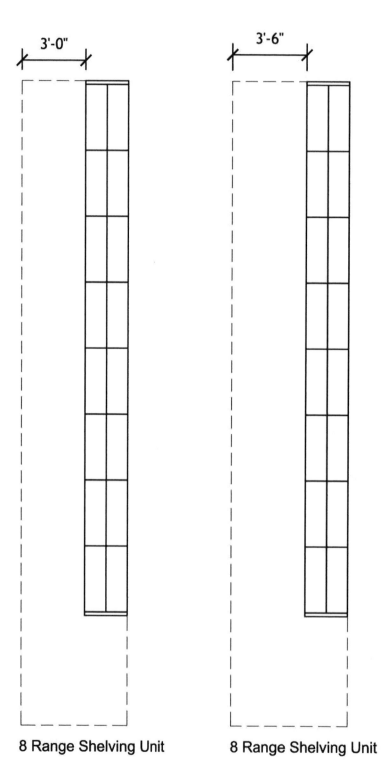

3'-0"

3'-6"

8 Range Shelving Unit   8 Range Shelving Unit

0   2'   4'   8'
SCALE 1/4"= 1'−0"

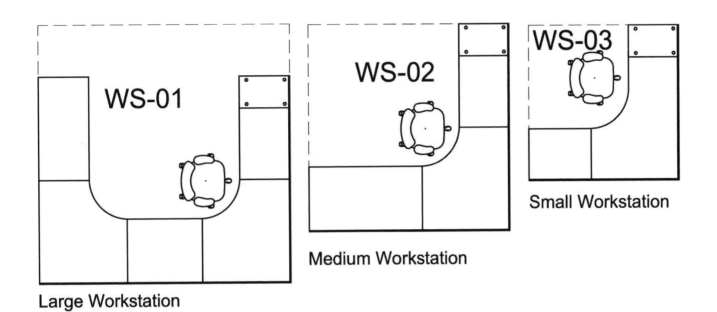

WS-01

Large Workstation

WS-02

Medium Workstation

WS-03

Small Workstation

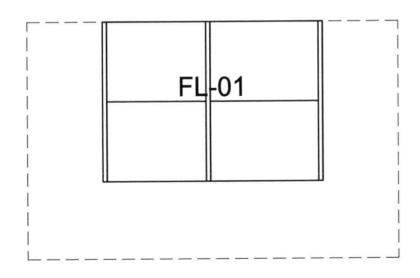

FL-01

AV Flipper Unit

0   2'   4'   8'
SCALE 1/4"= 1'-0"

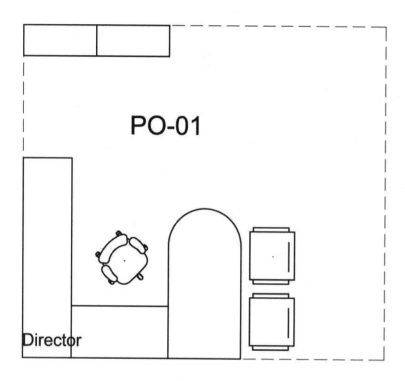

PO-01

Director

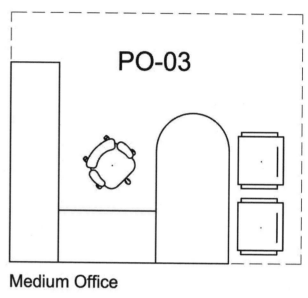

PO-03

Medium Office

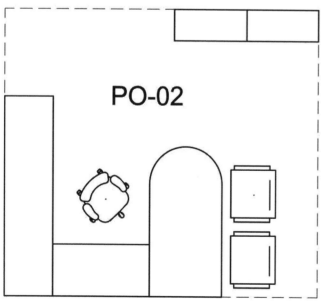

PO-02

Large Office

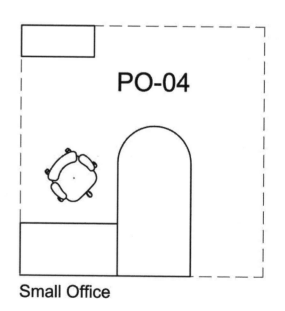

PO-04

Small Office

```
0        2'      4'              8'
SCALE  1/4"= 1'-0"
```

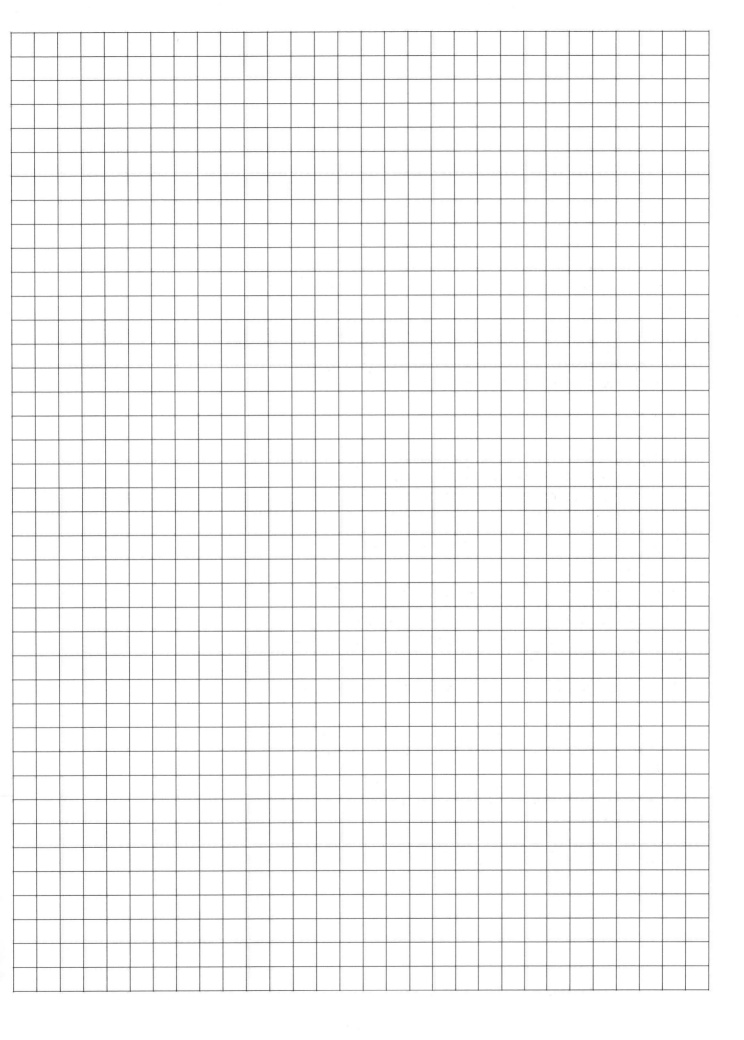

Bazillion, Richard J. and Braun, Connie L. Academic Libraries as High-Tech Gateways: a Guide to Design and Space Decisions. Chicago: ALA, 2001.

Provides tools for planning and building an academic library space of the future -incorporating the latest innovations in academic library facility design; being flexible for changing information technology needs; and balancing design, comfort and physical space demands.

Bolan, Kimberly. Teen Spaces: the Step-by-step Makeover. Chicago, ALA, 2009.

From analysis and planning to design and decoration, Bolan outlines the steps to take and the pitfalls to avoid when planning a teen-space project. Plentiful photographs and sidebars from librarians add to the depth of knowledge presented here.

Brown, Carol R. Interior Design for Libraries: Drawing on Function and Appeal. Chicago: ALA, 2002.

Focusing on functionality and appeal, this illustrated how-to guide offers a plan for designing new or renovated spaces. Provides information on how to incorporate technology, design for different age groups and areas of the library, facilitate the work of library users, and provide optimal access to the library's products and services.

Bryan, Cheryl. Managing Facilities for Results (PLA Results series). Chicago, ALA, 2009.

Concentrates on carving out new service areas within existing spaces in public libraries. Illustrates how to prioritize new services that need space; make plans and identify an appropriate location; present your case to funding authorities; conduct a "gap analysis"; find resources to reallocate and see what new items are needed; and identify building professionals to assist with alterations.

Erikson, Rolf and Markuson, Carolyn. Designing a School Library Media Center for the Future. Chicago, ALA, 2009.

Covers researching, planning, constructing, and moving into a new school media center. Useful diagrams include a progress flow chart, a bubble diagram, and flat and three-dimensional architectural sketches. Excellent appendixes include architectural symbols; space allocations and adjacencies; sample data forms; shelving, table, and chair measurements; and furniture specifications and manufacturers.

Jaramillo, George R., ed. Space Planning In Libraries. Spec issue of Colorado Libraries 32.1 (2006): 3-27.

Articles include: Space: the future frontier for librarians; The Library as learning environment: space planning in an academic library; Planning public libraries for today...and tomorrow; Designing the twenty-first century library; and Sight, sound & supervision: space planning for K-12 Library Media Centers.

Libris Design. U.S. Institute of Museum and Library Services. 10 October 2006 http://www.librisdesign.org/.

Libris Design is a library facility planning information system which includes a website with a trial version of the Libris Design database - a Microsoft Access database which can be used to create library building programs and furniture and equipment cost estimates, plan renovations, and produce budgets for library building projects. Users tailor generic library models into building programs for their own specific projects.

Leighton, Philip D. and Weber, David C. Planning Academic and Research Library Buildings. 3rd ed. Chicago: ALA, 2000.

Exhaustive guidebook to the planning and construction process from start to finish. Includes sketches, charts, an excellent glossary, and a much needed index..

Lushington, Nolan. Libraries Designed for Users. New York: Neal-Schuman Publishers, 2002.

Emphasizes the user's experience and how that should both inform and affect design decisions. The guide features numerous illustrations of library plans and equipment in order to demonstrate the variety of solutions to design issues.

McCabe, Gerard B. and Kennedy, James R., eds. Planning the Modern Public Library Building. Westport, CT: Libraries Unlimited, 2003.

22 essays offering insight into current activities in the area of building planning. Topics include space design; collection marketing; furniture selection, accommodating different age groups; technology; and more. Bibliographic essay appended.

McCarthy, Richard. Managing your Library Construction Project. Chicago, ALA, 2009.

Overview filled with practical advice to understand key relationships and manage a complex process. Checklists and sample construction documents provide hands-on insights into the best practices in library construction and tools to do the job.

Murphy, Tish. Library Furnishings: a planning guide. Jefferson, N.C.: McFarland, 2007.

Topics covered include the installation of adequate (and stable) shelving; user-friendly seating arrangements; and plans for satisfying ever-increasing technological requirements. Appendices contain a number of checklists; evaluations of various work stations and seating options; ADA surveys; and electronic planning

Sannwald, William W. Checklist of Library Building Design Considerations. 5th ed. Chicago, ALA, 2009.

The Checklist consists of 1500 questions on nearly every aspect of the library building project, from choosing a consultant to planning the dedication ceremony. Evaluate current space, identify ADA requirements, and track decisions as the building progresses. Meant to be used as a working document throughout the project the Checklist is appropriate for all types of libraries.

Acknowledgements

Committee members 1986- 1995 who worked on the first edition of Building Blocks:

Carol Anderson	Helmut Hutter	Emelie J. Shroder
Deborah B. Babel	Florence M. Mason	Matthew J. Simon
Joseph W. Barnes	David L. Michaels	Charles R. Smith
Anders C. Dahlgren	David C. Milling	Dennis E. Smith
Deborah B. Dancik	Annette M. Milliron	Lynn R. Smith
Mary Dale Deacon	Dale. S. Montanelli	Donald G. Sweet
Ruth Ann Fraley	Arthur P. Morgan	Lamar Veatch
Mary M. Gilles	Richard W. Murphy	Stanley J. Wilder
Merri A. Hartse	Gloria J. Novak	Julia A. Wood
H. Harrison Heath	Karen A. Nuckolls	Janice Skinner Yeager
William Hidell	Sheryl B. Owens	Michael Ann Zemon
Edgar L. Hillsman	Walter W. Pennington	
Anne S. Hudson	Pal V. Rao	

Committee members 1986- 1995 who worked on the second edition of Building Blocks:

Frank Allen	Helmut Hutter
Marie L. Clark	Michael J. LaCroix
Anthony M. Dos Santos	Anita Laruy
E. Christian Filstrup	Marilyn P. Lewis
Jerold W. Fine	Manuel Marti
Joseph H. Green	David L. Michaels
Steven W. Hagstrom	Virginia Moreland

Acknowledgements, continued

Barbara Norland

Phillip W. Ritter

Robert E. Schnare

D.W. Schneider

Janice G. Skinner

Elizabeth Gay Teoman

Committee members 2000- 2009 who worked on the third edition of Building Blocks:

Elinor Barrett

Scott Britton

Diane Bruxvoort

Laura J. Isenstein

Ellen E. Kardy

Gail Kennedy

Karen Kinney

James C. Lutz

Mary McLaren

Kent E. Miller

Judy E. Myers

Jean Annette Pec

Daria F. Pizzetta

James E. Richard

Margaret M. Sullivan

Denelle C. Wrightson

Special thanks to the many intern architects at H3 Hardy Collaboration Architecture for their tireless effort to assemble the 3rd Edition of Building Blocks.